Prophecy Now

**What God Is Saying About The Future And
What You Can Do About It**

Jason

Order this book online at www.trafford.com
or email orders@trafford.com

Most Trafford titles are also available at major online book retailers.

Printed in the United States of America.

ISBN: 978-1-4669-5587-5 (sc)
ISBN: 978-1-4669-5588-2 (e)

Library of Congress Control Number: 2012916220

Trafford rev. 09/06/2012

 www.trafford.com

North America & international
toll-free: 1 888 232 4444 (USA & Canada)
phone: 250 383 6864 ♦ fax: 812 355 4082

CONTENTS

INTRODUCTION

The purpose of this book is to hopefully enlighten the reader. I would like to relay to the reader guidance and information that I have received through prophetic dreams. Some of these dreams may predict future events and some may not. I simply want to impart the information giving my interpretations. Ultimately, it will be up to the reader to interpret the guidance for themselves and to decide whether it has merit for them personally or for the world in general. Time will tell how accurate it is.

Seeing the events and time frames haven't happened yet, it's anybody's guess as to whether events will transpire as predicted. However, many things that I have dreamed about have come true. This gives me reason to hope that I won't have gotten the interpretations or guidance completely wrong and that some of it, hopefully most of it, will be reliable.

Edgar Cayce, arguably one of the twentieth century's most accurate prophets, was not 100% accurate. He was more accurate than not, however. It has been estimated by some that he was approximately 90% accurate. If he was living today and he was 90% accurate, the media would be pounding down his door for predictions and so would the general public.

I can't tell you how accurate things will turn out to be but if the guidance found in this book is even half right, I'd feel very good about that. I'd chalk up the part that was wrong to misinterpretation or our ability to change outcomes once we become aware of those possible outcomes. The problem isn't with God, it's always with us on some level.

WHO IS JASON?

My real name is not Jason. The name was given to me in a dream. In the dream, God spoke to me and told me, "From now on, you will be known as Jason."

In the bible, God changed the name of Abram to Abraham so it's not unprecedented that God would give someone a new name. I wondered why I was given a masculine name when I am a female. There are very few females with the name Jason. One explanation could be that we may be male or female in our physical bodies but the soul or spirit outside of the body may not have a gender. It may also be that we are a perfect balance between both the male and the female in our spirit forms like the yin and the yang.

I am about 99% vegetarian and about 80% vegan. I'd be 100% vegetarian except for all the people eating meat around me and sometimes I get the run off from that, if you know what I mean.

I recently watched some of the documentary called, 'Earthlings' on Youtube. I recommend that any adult watch it. I think many of us have the idea that animals used for food are mostly happily frolicking around grassy hills on a farm and they live this way until they are humanely slaughtered. Unfortunately, this is not the reality.

In the garden of Eden, we were given the responsibility for caring for God's green Earth and all the creatures in it. At some point, we lost track of our role and our purpose. We lost our respect for our fellow creatures and decided that might is right. We decided that because they were weaker, we had the right to conquer and torture them. We no longer believed that they were entitled to enjoy their lives or enjoy this great green Earth with us. God have mercy on the animals we use for food because most of them rarely see the light of day, let alone enjoy the green grass, swim in, or drink from, our streams and lakes or fly free through the great blue sky. Most of them don't get to live a good and happy life. We made them our slaves, took away their sunshine and joy and in many cases, make them suffer on a daily basis until we finally kill them off to serve our selfish purposes. We throw our dependent pets out on the streets to die. We even kill our own unborn children. We've lost touch with our hearts and our ordained purpose as the caretakers of this planet.

Jesus said the whatsoever a man sows, that shall he reap. So, if an alien race were to arrive on Earth in spaceships and conquer us and turn us into their food supply in the same way we have used the animals of this planet, it would be just and fair. I'm not predicting this as an actual event to happen in the future. I'm just saying, think about it. I mean, really think about it! If you were about to become the main course on the menu and the tables were turned, so to speak, you would not be sitting on the fence. You'd be absolutely sure that the aliens were wrong, immoral and evil to do that to YOU! . . . 'you' being the operative word. You wouldn't think aliens were justified in eating you because they were stronger and smarter and had more advanced technology. Might wouldn't be right in yours eyes at that point, would it? But in the world of animals used for food, YOU are the wrong, immoral and evil alien! If it really is true that what comes around goes around as Jesus said, then what kind of a karma are we setting ourselves up for as a species? Could we reap what we sow by an alien race coming to Earth to eat us? The answer is 'yes.' It's called 'karma.' If karma exists, and if you believe the words of Jesus about reaping what you sow, it does, then let's avoid this karma and change our way of thinking and acting, shall we? Karma can come back in many forms but lets not choose actions that could attract an alien race of carnivores. Let's just learn this lesson of love before some harsh reality forces us to face ourselves.

People may not understand the personality of God, the Father. He loves all of His creations and He does not like people hurting His creations. The bible says, in Luke 12: 6-7, "6Are not five sparrows sold for two farthings, and not one of them is forgotten before God? 7But even the very hairs of your head are numbered. Fear not therefore: ye are more valuable than many sparrows."

My question is, "Exactly how many sparrows is one human being worth in God's tabulation?" Ten? Twenty? How many chickens? What if you are only worth 30 chickens to God but you have eaten thousands of chickens in your lifetime? Make no mistake. God loves the birds that He created. How important do you really think you are and how willing are you to bet your life on it before God?

I used to feed pigeons outside of my house. I also rented out rooms and ran a small business from inside of that house. The pigeons would poop on the steps leading into my house. It was a problem because if you are trying to run a business or rent rooms, people might not like to walk on steps covered in bird poop. So, I would go out daily and sometimes more often, to throw a bucket of soapy water on the poop to soften it and wash it away. I got tired of doing this. My Dad and brother came over and set up some nails on the roost where they were sitting above the steps to try to discourage them from pooping. This didn't work because then the birds just sat directly on the steps and pooped. The birds weren't getting the message.

So, I decided to quit feeding the birds. It was summer. I figured they could go out to the fields and get some grains or something and find another source of food.

I had a dream and in the dream, God was angry with me for not feeding the birds. When I woke up, I had quite a conversation about it, both with God and with myself. Should my time be wasted daily having to put out food and clean up poop on a continual basis? Isn't my time more valuable then spending it catering to a bunch of messy birds? Apparently, not in God's eyes. I suppose God was trying to teach me about my role in caring for His creations and my importance in the scheme of all things created. I was learning that I am not so important as I think I am. Consider the possibility that neither are you. Consider that the Holy Spirit chose to take the form of a dove when he baptized Jesus. That's a bird.

God is watching how we treat His creatures. They really do matter to Him. I did continue to feed the birds but I slowly cut back in the amount of food until I weaned them down. Shortly thereafter, the city asked people to quit feeding the pigeons and then I think that the city or somebody secretly or maybe not so secretly, poisoned a lot of them and killed a lot of them off. I guess the poop problem was a city wide problem. I was very upset when the birds died. I'm sure God was too. If He had been able to get His way, I'm sure He would have told the whole city that cleaning up after His birds was plenty good enough for them. We are full of our own self importance. Be very careful anytime you think you are better or more worthy or more valuable to God than any of God's other creatures. You may be in for a surprise. You may have to face some unpleasant karma. These other creatures matter very much to God.

I'll try to not make this a chip on my shoulder or to dwell excessively on this but we were vegan in the garden of Eden. Jesus told us to go and preach the gospel to all creatures.

Mark 16: 15, 'And he said unto them, Go ye into all the world and preach the gospel to every creature.' What kind of gospel are we teaching these creatures as we torment them, murder them and then chow down on them? Meat wasn't allowed to be eaten until after Noah's flood when the vegetation had all been destroyed by the water. Presumably, once the trees and plants came back, we should have reverted back to our original diet. Do you really think our digestive tracts and entire systems changed to eat animal products in that short period in time? Science repeatedly leads us to the conclusion that eating animal products creates conditions of ill health in our bodies. So at least think about returning to the original diet. The bible says that eventually the lion will lie down with the lamb or that the two will no longer be enemies. Maybe lions didn't eat lambs in the garden of Eden either and this will be a return to the original intention of creation.

I know there are many people who may disagree with me on this point but I really don't believe we can attain the highest level of spirituality when we, as a planet and as individuals, are so disrespectful of the Creator's other creatures. We are polluting our bodies and fogging up our supernatural senses and putting ourselves at odds with our creator. I don't think you can have a great communion with your Creator while you are hurting His other creations.

All of this started out being about 'Who is Jason?' so I'm going to continue with that. I don't know why I have been given the name Jason. I looked up possible meanings for the name and found that it means 'healer.'

My mother was a prophet. My father was a faith healer. My mother's prophecies were accurate. My father prayed for many, many people over the decades who were miraculously healed. He also had the gift of being able to see visions of what was wrong with people physically, mentally and spiritually. Many times he told people what was wrong with them before they told him, often confirming the diagnosis of doctors. If I ever felt sick, I'd just call him up on the phone and ask him to pray for me. He could give me the diagnosis and the cure in one phone call. I was never seriously sick a day in my life.

If I gave you my parent's names, you would probably not have heard of them. There are varying reasons for this. One reason is that they felt that their gifts were something that should not be profited from financially. They wanted to serve God with their gifts. While I don't think there would have been anything wrong with either of them or both of them having ministries that were profit producing, they had their own feelings and opinions about this. They didn't advertise. They wanted God to bring to them whoever He wanted them to help and God did.

If you understand the personality of God, the Father, you would understand that He wants each person to seek Him themselves. In fact, each of us was created as a companion for God. He doesn't want us to be looking at the great miraculous gifts of men and women and following after them. So, to a great extent, all of us must commune with God on our own if we want to receive from heaven. This is why so many miracles seem to happen without pomp and ceremony. It's almost as if God wants to hide His greatest miracles and His most talented servants from the general public. He doesn't want people to be following after the miracles or the people God uses to perform those miracles. Believe me, those people did not have anything to do with the actual miracles. It was all God's doing. We are not to make idols out of mere mortals. What those people did was get in line with God. God loves all of His creations and when they seek Him, He is happy to be found. God could use a donkey to perform a miracle . . . in fact, He did on the road to Damascus. The most that anyone can do for you is to point you in the right direction, towards God, the Father. The seeking and finding is up to you.

THE PROBLEM WITH THE NEW AGE MOVEMENT

If you do want to seek and find God and receive guidance for yourself, I recommend that you seek the highest source of guidance. That would be God, the Father, through the power of the Holy Spirit in the name of Jesus Christ. People who seek other guides may find themselves deceived or at least, they have gone with a lesser or inferior source when they could have gone straight to the source of all. Why not go straight to your creator? All other sources of guidance are inferior to Him.

This is the main problem with the New Age Movement. Some people believe they can do it all by themselves without God, the Father or the Holy Spirit or Jesus Christ. There is a belief system out there where people believe that they are all Gods and equal to God. This was the mistake that Lucifer made when he fell from heaven and a third of heaven left with him believing the same lie. Lucifer believed that because he was one with God, that this meant that he was equal to God.

God the Father is the creator of all. Everything, including you, was created by Him. He is the glue that holds the universe together. If God, the Father, could withdraw from all of creation, all of creation would cease to exist. We can be one with God but that doesn't mean that we are equal to God. No one and nothing is equal to God, not even Jesus or the Holy Spirit.

Jesus asked in Mathew 19: 17, "Why calleth me good? There is none good but one, that is, God."

He also said, in John 13: 16, "Verily, verily I say unto you, the servant is not greater than his lord; neither he that is sent greater than He that sent him."

Both Jesus and the Holy Spirit were sent by God, the Father, therefore; according to Jesus' words, neither Jesus nor the Holy Spirit can be greater than God, the Father, who sent them. Jesus was saying that He is not equal to God. Jesus was saying, I will not make the same mistake that Lucifer made believing himself to be equal to God. Jesus was saying that all good comes from God. If we have any good in us, it's because God's goodness has been created in us. Many people may not believe that Jesus and the Holy Spirit are not equal to God. Many people believe they are one and by being one, they are the same person and equal. I guess I'm stepping on a few toes here. I hope we can agree to disagree here. It is not what is traditionally taught in Churches about the Godhead. It is however, what I believe. It is what Jesus taught us while He was on Earth.

In John 14: 28, Jesus said, "You have heard how I said unto you, I go away, and come again unto you. If ye loved me, ye would rejoice, because I said, I go unto my Father: <u>for my Father is greater than I</u>."

It seems pretty clear to me that Jesus meant what he said. Disagree if 'ye' must. Just as long as you don't believe that you are equal to God or greater than God and thereby you believe you can do it yourself without God. That would be faulty thinking that would put you on the wrong track spiritually.

In my opinion, both the Church and the New Age Movement are in error when they believe that any spirit or any creation of God is equal or even greater than Him. If there is any message I would like to convey, it's that we can not do it without God, the father, and His servants who were sent to help us, the Holy Spirit and Jesus Christ.

I do believe that we are baby Gods struggling to mature and learn our lessons. Even Jesus agreed with this concept. In John 10: 34, Jesus answered them, "Is it not written in the law, I said, Ye are Gods."

The scripture He was referring to was in Psalms 82: 6, "I have said, Ye are gods; and all of you are children of the most high."

Nevertheless, no matter how God like the image was that you were created in or how God like and one with God you may become, you will never be equal to God, the Father or God, the creator of all. More importantly, you will never be able to defy His rules or His laws or be allowed to get away with your defiance for long without consequences. You will not be able to do anything apart from Him and what He allows. You can't move an arm or a leg or search one brain cell for information without His life force flowing through you. I assure you, He is a real personality and a real entity and you will never be equal to Him. If you continue to think that you are equal to Him, you will be caught in the lie that caused Lucifer's fall from heaven. If you want to go back to heaven, you can't be deceived about this. Jesus said he wasn't equal to God, the Father, and if Jesus wasn't equal to God, how can any of us believe that we will ever be equal? Who are you going to believe? Jesus or somebody else?

Some people think that Jesus was speaking as a man here and when he was resurrected, everything changed. I don't believe that Jesus would make himself into a liar just by dying. If the subject needed more explanation, I think He would have expanded on it. He would have had to clarify that once he was dead and reunited with God, the Father, He would then become one with Him and equal to Him. He would have had to explain that what He was saying while still on earth speaking as a man was going to change and would no longer be true at a later date. Jesus didn't explain it away. I believe He meant what He said.

Part One

WHAT IS GOD SAYING?

THE FREE TRADE AGREEMENTS

Many years ago, right around the time that Brian Mulroney was signing the first free trade agreement in 1987, I went to sleep at night and I had a dream.

The dream was as follows:

God was seated on his throne. He was like the brightest, white, shining spot light that obscured the details of his appearance. I could only see His silhouette in the shape of a man with long hair and a beard.

And then He spoke. "I don't like the Free Trade Agreement."

Then, He showed me many politicians, particularly politicians from Quebec, sound asleep at their desks.

Then, He spoke again. He told me that this agreement would hurt people, hurt industries and He specifically mentioned beef farmers. End of the dream.

I know I had my rant about all of us converting to a garden of Eden vegan diet. Yet, in this dream, God was concerned about the beef farmers. It seems like a bit of a contradiction. I think God is both an idealist and a realist. Yes. It would be better for our health and be kinder to animals and even improve the environment and ultimately, feed more people if we converted to being vegan. On the one hand, that is the healthiest diet originally designed by God for us. Nevertheless, God is concerned with all aspects of life. If meat eating just suddenly stopped, some people would lose their livelihoods and some people might even starve. God is concerned about all these things. I can also tell you that I was instructed through a vision to not make the meat eating issue a big chip on my shoulder. There is the ideal diet and then there is the reality that exists in the world and God is concerned with both.

I would like to be able to fully explain all the details of the Free Trade Agreement, FTA, and the subsequent one, NAFTA and why God doesn't like the Free Trade Agreements, but I'm not an expert on this topic. I did try to research it at the time I first received the dream.

At that point in my life, I was in my 20's and I knew practically nothing about politics. I thought politics was boring and for stuffed shirts. I didn't read the newspapers a whole lot and I wasn't particularly interested in the news. I picked my politicians by looking at the national or provincial leaders' debates and whoever I liked the most, that's who I voted for. Of course, this isn't any way to pick a leader. Even Hitler could put on a good show for a couple of hours but nevertheless, that's how I picked them. I was even less discerning when it came to municipal elections. Whoever took the time to arrive at my door, got my vote. I knew nothing about the issues.

I did believe in God. I had prayed to Him for years. I did believe that there was a possibility that the conversation could actually be two sided if there really was a real 'God.' I decided that God had indeed spoken to me. However, I didn't feel I was in a position to do anything about the message I had been given. I decided to take the prayer route. I prayed that God would wake up the politicians and enlightened the public and further reveal to me what He didn't like about the Free Trade Agreement.

I did learn some things about the FTA and NAFTA, the North America Free Trade Agreement, that would explain why God might not like these deals. In Chapter 11 of NAFTA, corporations are given citizen status. They may now sue governments for proposed losses of income due to any action of that government, even when that government is trying to protect it's other 'citizens.'

The Ethyl Corporation sued the Canadian federal government in the late 1990s when it tried to ban a substance in it's gasoline called MMT. MMT is believed to be harmful when inhaled particularly for children and the elderly because it may cause the slowing down of motor functions in the body.

The Ethyl Corporation won that lawsuit and Canadian taxpayers paid $25 million dollars in the settlement. They didn't win their court case because they proved that MMT wasn't harmful. They won because the Canadian government couldn't prove that it wasn't.

Under NAFTA, corporations don't necessarily have to pay for their own research anymore. They can just make the government pay for those studies for them. If taxpayers won't fund the research, then the companies can win and collects their lottery prizes. MMT is still in our gas all these years later. However, due to the public outcry, MMT is being slowly fazed out of gasoline. It's too bad that the government was helpless under NAFTA to stop it from coming into our environment in the first place. The point is that governments should have the right to ban potentially harmful substances for no other reason than it may be potentially harmful to its citizens. The companies bringing in potentially harmful products should pay for the research themselves and be forced to prove that their products are safe. It should not be the obligation of the government through taxpayer's dollars to prove that products are safe.

Our natural resources used to belong to Canada and to Canadians controlled by our provincial and federal governments. Under NAFTA, most Canadian natural resources can be sold to the buyers with the most money. Do you have millions or billions of dollars to buy up Canadian resources, develop them to make a profit for yourself? It's your right under NAFTA but most Canadian citizens just don't have that kind of money lying around. So, who gets to buy up everything? Large corporations. Also, foreign governments.

Prices are now set outside of the local situation. So, if you have corn growers in Ottawa who faced a flood or drought, prices can not be set to help them out, at least not legally under NAFTA. That would be playing favourites and the government can be sued. It's so much better if they can't compete and go out of business under the rules of NAFTA. As a matter of fact, some crop growers have ended up selling their crops for less than it cost them to produce due to the unfairness of NAFTA pricing and some do indeed, go out of business. Farmers have lost control over their own destinies under NAFTA.

President Obama has been advocating that Americans should buy American goods and services. This is really not acceptable under NAFTA, but nevertheless, it's a great idea. If you view the shipping containers at American and Canadian ports, you might become aware of the problem fairly evidently. There are millions of more shipments of imports coming into North America from China, then exports going out of North America to the rest of the world. Dollar by dollar, China is taking our money away from us. When you buy at home, you support jobs and local businesses. The money stays here and supports our industries. When we purchase products from China, we are supporting communism and hurting our own people and industries. Do you think that God would want you supporting communism, with its anti-religion and anti-God government policics? With dollars from around the globe, we are collectively making China one of the wealthiest nations in the world. You are voting with your money and it's time to ask yourself, "What am I voting for with my money?" It is time to buy at home. Under NAFTA, this is called favouritism. Nevertheless, it still makes enormous sense to buy products and services at home. Yes. You may be able to buy something cheaper if it is produced in another country because they can always undercut the price of our goods and services with cheaper labour, etc. Eventually, it will have an effect on our economy . . . like right now. So, buy locally. It's the best way that individuals can help the economies of their countries. A little saving of money now, isn't worth the lost jobs or a sharp drop in the standard of living. Countries like China are buying up our countries' resources out from underneath us and they are doing it with our own money that we are giving to them.

Oil and gas could be taken from Alberta and sold to Canadians at a cheaper rate than elsewhere in the world to help with a recession . . . but wait, no it can't. For the most part, we can't count on collectively owning our oil reserves anymore through various levels of government. Some companies from France, China, Korea, Norway, United States and England, among others, now own stakes in our oil industry.

It's better that we all struggle through recessions or depressions to preserve world prices, potentially fund terrorism and give the middle east the right to hold us over a barrel . . . . when we have all the oil that any nation could ever need to last us probably hundreds of years. However, under NAFTA, corporations can now own our Canadian supply. We can't set the price of our oil and gas or even have the right to collectively own it and control it under NAFTA. The average citizen doesn't really seem to exist as a citizen anymore and levels of government don't really exist as levels of government protecting Canadians and our resources anymore. Corporations control the government and we citizens exist mostly as consumers for corporations to sell us our resources back to us after they took them from us under NAFTA. If you are not on some pharmaceutical drug or purchasing some product that the corporations are peddling, then the corporations don't need you, do they? The whole system under NAFTA is like a snake eating it's own tail.

The whole national treatment clause in NAFTA was a bill of rights drafted for large corporations. The average citizen was not being considered beyond how could they take our natural resources away from us through our governments and leave us sitting ducks for any harmful substance that may come down the turnpike. They succeeded. We've been fleeced and most people don't even know what they've lost or what is still at stake. Unfortunately, when big business takes over, citizens and the environment are not given much consideration. Environmental and social issues can only get worse.

Under NAFTA, no province can allow a corporation to bulk sell its water without every province being forced to do it. If one company anywhere is allowed to take our water in bulk, then EVERY company that wants to, must be allowed to buy and sell our water too. Otherwise, it would be favouritism at work and these corporations could sue the government for proposed lose of income. Not actual loss of income but proposed (without actually having to put out the normal expenditures of time and money or do the work to make those profits). Under NAFTA, once water is sold in bulk, it would become a commodity. If this door ever opens, our water supply could literally be drained right out from under us. Under NAFTA, the needs of Canadians for our water is secondary to the needs of these greedy corporations so they get the water first. This makes perfect sense if you are a corporation wanting to buy and sell water. It makes no sense at all if you are a Canadian citizen or an American citizen who expects to have water to drink throughout your lifetime or if you think the wildlife or the ecosystems of waterways are important.

You have to wonder why we shouldn't be able to allow one company to buy and sell bulk water while not allowing another. The water supply is not endless yet it is being treated under NAFTA as if it is. This decision, like so many others, should be in the hands of citizens through their democratically elected governments that most people believed were elected to protect their interests. Under NAFTA, this will not always be possible as any decision to help one individual or one business or one industry can be challenged in court and overturned. Worse than this is the opening of the flood gates to an endless sea of corporations pillaging our resources. All corporations that would like to, must be allowed under NAFTA, to pillage our resources equally.

Glaciers above Europe and around the world are drying up at an alarming rate. Europe's glaciers have lost approximately 25% of their mass within the last decade alone. Scientists are predicting these glaciers could be completely gone in 10-30 years from now. When they disappear, don't be surprised to see our lakes and rivers drained of water too. It could happen. Under NAFTA, you don't really own much of anything and you really don't have a right to much as a citizen anymore. Water will be the gold of the future and YOU probably don't own any or have a right to any of it. Let's hope you can still buy it. Think about that.

Trade between countries is a good thing. They might have goods and services that we want and need and vice versa. Free trade is a good thing but the FTA and NAFTA are not good deals for the average citizen. I recommend you research more about this. It may sound like crazy talk to you right now but with research, it may become clearer to you that what I am saying is true.

My Dad had a dream many years ago. He saw lakes in Canada completely drained of water. Let's hope it was just a nightmare. Under NAFTA and with the shrinking supply of fresh safe water on a worldwide basis, sadly, it could become a reality.

RWANDA

In 1993, I had a dream. In the dream, I was told to pray for a country called Rhonda or what sounded like Rhonda.

When I awoke, I did search for the country Rhonda on the internet. I couldn't find it. I asked everyone I knew if they had ever heard of a country called Rhonda. No one had. I couldn't come up with anything. Maybe I didn't try hard enough.

At one point I remember thinking that even if it was a country on another planet, I was determined to do as the dream directed me to do and pray. So I did.

In 1994, there was a major tragedy in a country called Rwanda. A tribe called the Hutu attacked another tribe called the Tutsis. Almost a million Tutsis were murdered by being chopped up with machetes. One participant in the genocide said he felt like a spirit or presence over took him and he was caught up in the moment and he killed his neighbours along with other Hutus. Deep seated hatred and prejudice were at the root of the massacre.

After the event, there were healing circles where members of the Hutus who participated in the murders, met with the surviving Tutsis to try to reconcile with their neighbours. They literally were neighbours living beside one another so it wasn't like the two groups could move to either side of the country to avoid one another. It is a miracle that they could sit down together or even communicate with one another at all. How would you like to sit down and forgive people who chopped up and murdered your Dad, your Mom, your sister, your brother, your wife, your husband, your son or your daughter? Some of the survivors had hatchet wounds and were missing body parts like legs and arms. The Tutsis could sure teach us in North America a thing or two about forgiveness and reconciliation. The country and all it's citizens still need to heal. Please join me in continuing to pray for Rwanda.

Dear God:

"Let the peace and love and forgiveness of Jesus Christ permeate through every heart of the people of Rwanda. Please heal their land. Lord. Let your angels walk the streets and guard the peace of Rwanda. We ask this through the power of the Holy Spirit in the name of Jesus Christ. Amen."

PRESIDENT BARACK OBAMA

Strangely, I was only asked in dreams to pray for specific things a few times in my life. One time was when I was instructed in a dream to pray for Rwanda. Later, I was instructed in a dream to pray from President Barack Obama.

Unfortunately, the dream didn't say specifically what to pray for. In my dream, it seemed like there had been an attempt on the President's life which failed or at least he was injured. He seemed to have trouble with one of his knees and he had to walk with a cane afterwards until it healed. It looked like a marble type of flooring he was laying on. Maybe there was light gash on his forehead like a bullet or a knife had lightly penetrated the surface of his skin but not done any significant damage.

When I prayed about the dream, I saw visions of a castle. The castle was surrounded by a mote with a draw bridge. The draw bridge was drawn up because people were storming the castle. I thought this might mean that the people of the United States who are out of jobs and losing their houses and desperate for money, could end up rioting. There could be people shooting at each other in the streets. It may also be in reference to Israel.

I think the dream is important. The genocide in Rwanda was not a small thing. It was a major incident of unbridled evil being unleashed in the world. Likewise, I think President Barak Obama will be at the center of some major evil event to take place in the world if this event can't be prayed away.

I wonder if President Obama knows about God's covenant with Israel. The bible says that Israel is the apple of God's eye. When anyone takes a poke at Israel, they are poking God in his eye.

In Zechariah 2: 7-11, we read, 7Deliver thyself, O Zion, that dwellest with the daughter of Babylon. 8For thus saith the Lord of Hosts; After the glory hath he sent me unto the nations which spoiled you: ***for he that toucheth you toucheth the apple of his eye.*** 9For, behold, I will shake mine hand upon them, and they shall be a spoil to their servants: and ye shall know that the Lord of hosts hath sent me. 10 Sing and rejoice, O daughter of Zion: for, lo, I come, and I will dwell in the midst of thee, saith the Lord. 11And many nations shall be joined to the Lord in that day, and shall be my people: and I will dwell in the midst of thee, and thou shalt know that the Lord of hosts hath sent me unto thee. 12And the Lord shall inherit Judah his portion in the holy land, and shall choose Jerusalem again.

The apple of an eye is literally the eye ball. So whoever touches Israel is poking God in His eye. Now, would anyone really want to do that? Especially when the next verse of scripture says that God will shake his hand upon whoever pokes Him in His eye by touching Israel and He will make them a spoil to their servants.

When Jesus walked this Earth, he walked in the land of the bible, in Israel.

There is an interesting book called, 'He Walked the Americas.' This book describes tribal stories from many ancient American cultures regarding a man who had scars on his feet and hands. He wore a white robe with the design of crosses on the hem. The robe was like the kind of attire that Jesus would have worn in ancient Israel. According to the legends and myths, he walked all over America performing miracles and teaching the natives about love and peace and forgiveness. I mention this because some readers might find this an interesting read. Others might not.

That being said, when Jesus returns to Earth, the bible tells us that Jesus will return to the Mount of Olives in Jerusalem. He won't be touching down in New York, Paris, or Washington, DC. Israel and the Jews are still God's chosen people. Nothing has changed in that regard in spite of all that Jesus has done. Jesus was a Jew and the Jews are special in God's eyes.

I hope and pray that President Obama will have the wisdom to know that He can't divide any part of Israel without a major backlash upon himself and America. I honestly believe if America divides Israel, God will divide America. He could possibly do this with a massive earthquake that will split the nation in two as well as physically reshape the whole country. I hope that President Obama will not poke God in His eye. If he does, it will be America that pays for it as well as any other nation that joins in.

Unfortunately, I was not told specifically what to pray for regarding President Obama. I only know I was told to pray and pray I will. I also feel strongly in my spirit that whatever is needing prayer, is not an insignificant thing. It will be a major event or a series of events . . . . something as big as or bigger than almost a million people being hacked to death with machetes. President Obama may be at the helm of America, at the most challenging and trying time in all of its history. I could sum it up with one word. 'Trouble.' Terrible troubling times are on the way for America. Although, as always, through prayer and changing actions, any problem or series of problems can be changed or healed with the help of God, through the power of the Holy Spirit, in Jesus' name.

I hope that the economic principles expressed by Paul Hellyer and others, as discussed further in this book, will be considered and applied to help create jobs and wealth in the world and for the US. God showed me in a dream that He already had people with the solutions in place in positions in parliament and within governments and other important agencies. The solutions have been given and the people who could bring forward those proposals and solutions are already there. He said that many of them were afraid of being laughed at or ridiculed and even feared losing their jobs if they spoke up. It's time for governments and agencies to encourage their experts to speak up without fear of being ridiculed or fired. God has already provided the solutions. He needs His people to speak up and He needs government officials and the people in positions of power to be able to do something. They need to listen to God's solutions and act. I believe that some of these economic solutions that have been brought forward by Paul Hellyer, are divinely inspired. The devil controls the whole worldwide monetary system and God would like to change that. He knows how to bring about prosperity for the whole globe and He is prepared to do that, if people would only open their ears and listen. If people don't listen, the world will be like a snake eating it's own tail. Eventually, there will be a collapse. God has other ideas if only people would listen to Him.

Dear God:

"Please send many angels to watch over and protect President Barack Obama, his family and his staff. Please stand looking over the shoulder of President Barack Obama. Please impart to him your intuition, your wisdom and your good judgement to be applied to every decision that he makes. Open his eyes and soften his heart. Let the love of Jesus pour into and out of his heart. Show him in advance what will happen if he takes certain actions and caution him in advance. Bring the solutions that You have for America and the globe to his knowledge and to his attention. I can't think of many people who need Your help more than he does, with the weight of America and the world on his shoulders. Every move he makes can have so many ramifications that no one but You can know in advance what those ramifications will be. Please be his strong help, his strong guide and His strong deliverance in his time of need and meet his needs and the needs of the people. Only You can figure out what needs to be done and what the right courses of action are. President Obama is only a mortal man who needs divine assistance to deal with what is coming. Show him Your ways. If he doesn't know, show him how important Israel is to You and caution him not to poke You in Your eye. We ask this through the power of the Holy Spirit in the name of Jesus Christ. Amen."

TSUNAMI

I had a dream in 2004. I dreamed that I saw a long sunny beach with palm trees. I realized that all the water had been sucked off of the shoreline like what happens before a tsunami. I looked out to the ocean and there was a giant wall of water in the air. I saw a giant hand, the hand of God, holding the water suspended in the air. I knew in the dream that God was about to release the water and that a lot of people were going to die.

A few months later, the Indian Ocean Tsunami, also called the Boxing Day Tsunami, unleashed it's power. Over 230,000 people were killed. The earthquake which triggered it was the third largest earthquake ever recorded by a seismograph with a magnitude of 9.0. Apparently, the whole earth shook by at least 1 centimetre.

I know there are people who believe that natural disasters are just that; natural disasters and that God doesn't cause them and that He has nothing to do with them. Some people couldn't understand why a loving God would allow such a thing let alone be the cause of it. Only God knows why these disasters take place. It could be a warning for the survivors to change their ways and get right with God. Once a collective of people pass a certain level of evil activities and thoughts, the protection of God lifts off of that area of the globe. It may also be a test for the improvement of our souls. For whatever reason, they do happen. Collectively and individually, it seems that life is full of trials and tribulations. I am a person that believes that God is in control no matter what happens.

I also think that everything that God has made, both what we perceive as good and evil, have purposes under the sun. If they didn't serve God's purposes in some way, they wouldn't be here. What can teach you about good better than being exposed to evil and learning by comparison? For some people, this is the best way to learn the difference between right and wrong. How can you see what's wrong in yourself unless you meet someone just like yourself with traits that you can plainly now see need to be improved because they bug you so much in that other person? The bible is a good book but you could use it for evil purposes such as hitting people over the heads. People have been beaten, jailed and murdered just for owning a bible.

The bible tells us that some of what we think is good, God thinks is bad. Some things that we think of as bad, God thinks are good. We don't necessarily see things the way God does.

In regards to the guidance predicting this tsunami, I don't think it was particularly remarkable. I wasn't given a time frame for this event to take place. Eventually, there would have been a tsunami somewhere in the world making this prediction come true. It really couldn't fail. Not much a prediction at all although it was one of the largest ever recorded so that does make it a tiny bit remarkable.

GUN CONTROL LEGISLATION

I had a dream some time around the time that Canada was about to implement new gun control legislation. I had the dream prior to 2001 when the legislation was going to require that all guns be registered. In the dream, God said that he didn't like the gun control bill.

At the time, I wasn't entirely sure why God didn't like the gun control bill. Those who were opposed to the bill, mostly rural dwellers, had many arguments against it. They were angry that the government was targeting law biding citizens when the criminals were the ones committing the crimes with guns. Seeing that the criminals were illegally obtaining their guns in secrecy, they would still have their guns anonymously but there would be a record of all the law biding citizens who owned guns. It wasn't seen as much of a solution for curtailing crimes committed with guns like the government was promoting that it would be. Also, they thought it would be very expensive. It did turn out to be very expensive costing over a billion dollars and for that price tag, achieving very little gain. There were already lots of laws dealing with crimes committed with firearms and some people didn't feel more laws were needed. Some people were afraid that law biding citizens would be turned into criminals if they didn't register their guns. Some farmers wanted the right to have a gun to shoot a rabid fox that wandered in to attack his herds without having to go to take a course in how to own a gun, get a gun licence and a gun acquisition certificate with all the corresponding effort and expense. It was seen as a lot of trouble and another form of tax and control on citizens by the government.

However, I think the biggest overriding fear was that people were afraid that the government, once they knew where most of the guns were, would, at some point in time in the near or far future, take the guns away from the citizens. People were afraid of a war or a government takeover and they were afraid that they would not be able to defend themselves. Other people, mostly urban dwellers, just didn't like the idea of anyone having a gun at all and would have preferred it if all citizens could have been 'de-gunned, 'in the name of safety for all.

When I talk about future predictions for the globe a little bit further along in this book, I think the reasons will become more clear as to why God was against this bill and why He would be opposed to other similar bills being implemented in other countries. We are heading into a time of testing. There will be wars and some countries will be taken over. There is so little protecting the rights of citizens at the moment that besides God, guns may be our greatest personal asset and defence in the future. The terrorists and criminals have guns and no one knows who has them or how many guns or other weapons they may have. Why should law biding citizens be made more vulnerable and exposed than any of them? In wartime, this won't make sense. We live in a relatively peaceful country right now but will that last forever? I'm sorry to say, I don't think it will.

AIDS

When AIDS first appeared on the world's radar in the 1980s, the media was talking about it but no one was 100% sure what was the cause or how to contract it. People were being told it was a sexually transmitted disease but it was the fear of the unknown that really ostracised victims of AIDS. People were afraid to shake hands or sit on toilets.

At this time, I had a dream about AIDS. In the dream, I was shown the disease. It looked like a branch of a tree that had many other branches. It was dead without leaves and it was the colour of a white bone. I was told many things about the AIDS virus. I was told that it was a very powerful evil spirit or demon that was being allowed to come onto the planet for the first time. I was shown that through it's many branches, it could link up with other diseases and their corresponding demons and attack and kill its victims with more than just one disease at a time.

In the dream, I was shown people who were being tested for AIDS. Some of these people had the disease but were testing normal. It's called having a false negative result and it was not known about at the time that I had this dream. Then, I was shown that the disease could spread to cats and other animals. This was significant as far as guidance being correct because at that time, scientists were saying that it could not spread to animals. It wasn't until a few years later that they discovered the disease in cats. It's called Feline AIDS.

Then I was shown the plant life and I was made aware in the dream that AIDS could spread into plant life. As far as I know, no one is talking about the spread of AIDS to plant life so if scientists start talking about it, you'll have heard about it for the first time right here.

In the dream, I was shown the future. The immune systems of the plants were weakened by AIDS or an AIDS like immune deficiency. Both the animals and the crops were diseased and contaminated and there was very little left that was fit for humans to eat.

However, there was a way to survive. Christians would need to band together in groups. For each group, it would be necessary for three people from that group to fast and pray and read the bible on behalf of that whole group. After three days, another group of three people would take over for another three days, praying, fasting and reading the bible. This was the only way that the prayers would be powerful enough to defeat this demon.

The disciples of Jesus tried to cast a demon out a man but the demon wouldn't come out. In Mark 9: 28-29, the disciples asked Jesus why they couldn't cast the devil out. '28And when he was come into the house, his disciples asked him privately, Why could we not cast him out? 29 And he said unto them, "This kind can come forth by nothing, but prayer and fasting."

The demon of AIDS is one of those demons that can't be overcome without prayer and fasting. It's a new demon recently allowed on the planet for these end times and it is a powerful one.

MASS STARVATION

In another dream, I saw the landscape and it was full of dead grass and very little green grass. People were wandering looking for food. Some people were being forced to kill and cook their pets like their dogs and cats. Some people were so hungry, they were cooking and eating other people.

I assume if this happens, it will be near the very end just before Christ returns. This mass starvation may be caused by many factors as well as AIDS.

The terminator seed, developed and promoted by the Monsanto corporation as well as well the governments around the globe who are promoting it and will profit from it, may become a part of the termination of our food supply. Although I've never had a prophetic dream telling me this, I can't help but fear that if plants with the termination technology spread to other plants, it might have an adverse affect on the world's food supply. These plants are genetically engineered to not produce any seeds. About a billion people depend on replanting their saved seeds to live. About 80% of the world's farmers depend on their saved seeds to survive. If the terminator seeds replace plants whose seeds can be replanted, this may cause a massive die off of human beings even without the possibility of cross pollination. I can't be in agreement with any technology that has the possibility of starving the poor masses of this globe no matter how much money may be at stake. If the plants that have been genetically modified with terminator seeds cross pollinate with other food crops, this could result in a world with very few seeds to plant except terminator seeds. If these plants, for whatever reason, have or cause problems that translate into less crops, there could be a worldwide shortage of food crops. Diversity in food crops is very important to our survival.

The organic food market could also be under threat, not just from terminator seed technology and pesticide run offs but from other genetically modified plants that are cross pollinating. It's not possible to completely control or regulate this genetic pollution. It continues to spread. We need to tell the food industry that we want organic foods. The only way to do that is with our money. Buy organic. Don't fund the food industry that is bringing you pesticide laden foods and genetically modified foods unless you are in agreement with that.

Jesus said, "If they aren't against us then they must be for us." If you aren't against them then you must be for them. Do you want a healthier future? Then support the organic food industry if you like what they are doing to promote non genetically modified products and pesticide free, nutrient rich soil. Literally, put your money where you mouth is. Or, continue to fund the other food industry if that's what you want to do. If you choose to do that, just don't be surprised if organic is not an option for any of us at some time in the future. The organic industry will be as strong as the dollars that support it. I can see how people are spending their money and most people are supporting the pesticide industry and highly processed and nutrition-less foods and genetically modified foods.

When Prime Minister Chretien was Prime Minister of Canada, he ate organic foods at 24 Sussex Drive. I don't know the eating habits of the other PMs. I read that President Obama eats organic food at the White House. Michelle Obama decided to plant an organic garden at the White House. She's already in hot water with the pesticide industry. She has been called irresponsible for promoting locally grown organic foods. Some people want her to protect her garden with 'crop protecting products,' also known as pesticides.

I suppose you could argue that pesticides are necessary at the moment to fight some of the bugs that eat the crops. If the food industry had investigated other more natural options for pest control, then this might not be the case. If the demand for organic produce becomes stronger, then there may be much more research into natural healthy pest control. Decide what kind of future you want and spend your money accordingly.

Mass starvation is not a future that anyone can look happily forward to but there is a reason to hope for the future. Nothing is written in stone. The bible is full of predictions that could have come true but people repented and God changed His mind and gave them another chance. Mankind can change his future by changing his ways but will he? It is possible and we can try. In fact, in the dream about the dead grass and mass starvation, I was aware that I could make a difference to this possible future along with the efforts of other people. More on hope for the future further along in this book.

I remember hearing a story that Maude Barlow, the leader of the Council of Canadians, also had a dream about a future with mass starvation. This dream inspired her to get involved politically to try to alter this possible future reality. She's making a difference by influencing and linking together hundreds of thousands of Canadians to improve our environment and to improve government policies that affect the environment.

There are probably many, many people who have had prophetic dreams related to this. Some people just have an innate awareness that trouble is coming and that we need to try and change the outcome. I am sure there are a lot of us out there. There is hope if enough of us become aware and do something to bring about change.

THE DIAMOND OF EVIL

In 2005, I had a dream that God was looking down at a section of the US and British Columbia in Canada and he was planning on breaking off that section and sinking it into the ocean. He called the area, 'The Diamond of Evil.' I was shown the map of the US and I was allowed to look at the map for a short time to see the diamond of evil. I drew the area as accurately as I could remember on the map. The outline, including the dotted line area, makes the shape of a diamond with four points, one at the top, two at the sides and one at the bottom. The section that is outlined in a solid line is the part of the land that God is going to lop off into the ocean. Arizona appeared to be mostly left intact, although you can't tell this from the map. Also, the damage to the inland coast of Mexico extended further down than what the outline of the map indicates.

I'm not sure how far into the interior of the coast the point of the diamond goes. That's why I circled that area. It could be within the circle or include an even larger area.

When this will happen or what will cause it was not revealed to me. I think it may be caused by an earthquake or a bomb. It may be a bomb that triggers an earthquake or an earthquake that triggers a bomb. I think both a bomb and an earthquake will be involved.

Diamond of Evil

TERRORISTS

In 2004, I was given a directive in a dream. I was told to: "Get out of the city. Get off the beaten trail. People will be shooting at each other in the streets."

Through further prayer and asking for guidance, I was given other dreams which lead me to believe that there would be a terrorist attack in Ottawa. Also, I was shown that terrorist cells had already been set up in each of the provinces. I believe this is also happening in cities in the US. In my dream, there were 42 men per terrorist cell. I dreamed that they were smuggling bomb parts into Canada in automobiles by breaking the bombs down to their smallest components and hiding them behind metal plates in imported cars.

I had another dream that terrorists would target soft targets like specifically museums. I think they might also target things like bridges and malls.

In another dream I had in 2011 or 2012, I saw the statue of liberty lying on it's side in the New York harbour after a series of explosions knocked it over.

In another dream, I was screaming at politicians telling them how wicked and corrupt they were and that God was going to kill a lot of them.

This dream about politicians being killed makes me think of another couple of guesses about how this could come about or be averted altogether. The scenario of a lot of politicians being killed makes me think that terrorists could attempt or even succeed at a takeover of the Canadian government and actually occupy Parliament Hill by military force. How would Parliament Hill or 24 Sussex Drive hold up against hundreds or thousands of terrorists with guns and bombs converging on those locations? Are they adequately protected? It is my hope that someone who has the authority, will put improved contingency plans in place to protect Parliament, 24 Sussex or any other government offices that could be vulnerable. Perhaps just by having this book circulate and having people discuss these possibilities, it will have the effect of changing the outcome. If their plans are exposed and they lose the element of surprise, terrorists might change their plans. Or, maybe by hearing about these possibilities, those in authority to do so, will change their approach and avert a disaster. If the terrorists see that God has exposed their plans in advance then maybe they will also see that God really does speak to me and maybe other things that I am saying in this book are also correct. I hope and pray that they will receive Jesus as their saviour as a result of this book.

In another dream, I was driving into Brockville, Ontario. I saw a banner over the 401 at Brockville and it read, 'Southeastern Death Zone.' I saw bomb craters around Brockville. I think this dream was showing me that the whole of southern Ontario along the 401 (a very beaten trail) will be a hot spot for the fighting and 'shooting at each other in the streets.'

This dream supports the idea of the overthrow of our Canadian government by terrorist forces. The dream suggests fighting along the border between Canada and the US. If Canada was occupied by terrorists and the US wasn't, there would be fighting across the border.

In one dream, I was told that Canadians can't even imagine how bad it is going to be. This is a real nightmare because I can imagine some pretty horrible stuff happening. How bad is this thing going to be that we can't even imagine it?

In another dream, I was told that the real estate market was going to do a double collapse. I don't know what a double collapse is but I'm assuming it means interest rates will skyrocket and property values will plummet. In another dream, there was debate about who owned all the property. So many people had lost their properties that there was debate about whether the banks owned everything or if the people still had the right to live in their homes even if they couldn't make the mortgage payments. Sounds like now is the time to get out of debt, folks. Move into a trailer if that's all you can afford. It's better to live in a little trailer and own it then have the bank come and repossess your home.

In one dream, I was shown a power surge that went through the power lines and it caused the air conditioners and computers and most other electrical equipment to short out. I'm not sure if it was sent through the wires by the terrorists or if it was some freak overload or if it was a solar flare, but it destroyed a lot of technology.

Since having this dream, I heard Jack Van Impe on TV talk about how Iran was already working on a device that could send out an electrical surge that could wipe out a lot of technology. In a local newspaper, there was some reminiscing about the storm of 1989 that knocked out Hydro-Quebec's power grid. I thought it was just a storm because the media at that time said it was just a storm. Thousands of people were without electricity. Apparently, now they are saying it was caused by a solar flare, one of the largest magnetic storms ever recorded. What else aren't they telling us?

I had another dream in which I was told, "One in June. One in July." I woke up feeling that it could be terrorist attacks that would take place, one in June and the second wave in July, but I'm not entirely sure that I had prayed prayer protection over myself before sleeping and having that dream. The dream wasn't very clear about what it was referring to by 'one'. One what?

I saw a vision of the grime reaper and he was tapping his watch and looking at me sternly. I think it means the time is coming quickly. Although a year was not given, I have since had other dreams that may point to a time frame.

Possible Time Frames:

In another dream on December 21, 2008, I was told that there would be four years without trouble for some people. I would be one of the people who would be without trouble for seven years.

On December 21, 2012, the day the Mayan calendar ends, will be exactly four years from the date of my dream. I believe there will be a major event after that date. I believe that on December 21, 2012, one era will end and another era of testing will begin. Our last chance to clean up our acts and clean up our planet is being presented to us, as we lead up to the reign of the anti-Christ and the return of Jesus Christ.

I believe that after the seven year period ends on December 21, 2015, there will be a time of trouble for Canada and Canadians. I am assuming that I will still be living in Canada at the time as I don't have any aspirations at the moment to move to another country. I think the event will be more widespread than just Canada and could affect the whole world.

I am only guessing here but it's possible that if there is going to be a terrorist attack in Canada and North America, what better date for them to do it on then December 25th? The whole country will be shut down for the holidays and there won't be many people standing on guard. We'll all be gathered around our Christmas trees, opening presents or eating our Christmas feasts.

It's important to understand that the principles of democracy were formed out of Judeo-Christian theology. Democracy is all about respect for the individual's freedoms and rights and also ruled by the democratic vote of the majority. It encompassed the right to free speech, the right to assemble, the right to own property, the right to practice your religion, the right to not be persecuted for each individual's differences. Democracy is about the freedom to pursue happiness while living in harmony with your neighbours. It's about peaceful co-existence. I could go on here endlessly describing the Judeo-Christian principles of democracy that many people have fought and died to uphold for us. We value democratic principle. We must continue to be diligent to protect democracy or we could lose it.

What politicians and the general populations of democratic countries need to understand, is that Muslims do not aspire to our democratic principles. They are not of the Judeo-Christian faiths that inspired our democratic principles.

They do not want freedom of religion for anyone but themselves. When Mohammad tried to win over the Jews, at first there were loving verses in the Koran. When the Jews outright rejected Mohammad, he changed his tune. He then told his followers to try to convert them, but, if the don't convert, kill them. Kill the infidels. The infidels are the Jews and the Christians and the atheists. If we don't follow Allah, there is not much mercy for us in the Muslim religion. In a Muslim society, a Christian or a Jew has little respect or rights and they are routinely persecuted or worse, killed.

Lebanon is the prototype or the template of what is to come for other democratic countries that welcome in the Muslims in large numbers. Any country that aspires to multiculturalism, is particularly vulnerable. Muslims do not assimilate well into democratic societies.

Multiculturalism encourages them to retain their anti-democratic stance. Islam is not just a religion. It is a religion and a political movement and it is also a culture. It encompasses every area of a Muslim's life. We have moved away from religion in our politics. They want their religion in their politics. It is intrinsic to their religion and their way of life.

Lebanon was a democratic, predominantly Christian country with freedoms and rights for women. Lebanon began bringing small numbers of Muslims into Lebanon. However, Muslims had many more children then the general Lebanese population, and within 30-40 years, the Muslim population became the majority. As the majority, the Muslims elected a Muslim government. That Muslim government declared a Jehad on the Jews and the Christians within their borders and they slaughtered all the Jews and Christians, at least the ones who were unable to escape or hide in basements. They killed or chased out all the infidels and stole their possessions, their homes and their homeland.

Brigette Gabriel, now the head of an organization called, 'Act for America,' had to hide, as a child, with her parents in a neighbour's basement for years during the war in Lebanon, for fear of being killed by the Muslims. Her mission as an adult, is to stop the same thing from happening here in North America. She firmly believes the same events will reoccur here if we are not diligent to prevent it. I believe that she is correct in her assumption. The Muslim religion does not aspire to democracy and when given a democratic vote as a majority, they do not choose democratic principles or democratic governments. Any population that values its democratic society, should think long and hard whether it is worth the risk to bring in massive amounts of people who do not believe in the respect for the individual's rights or believe in the freedom of any religion or culture other than their own. Any country where the Muslim religion is dominant, the minority in other religions are oppressed and persecuted. Is that what we want in Canada and the US? I don't want to convert or die. As a woman, I sure don't want to wear a hejab or live under Sharia law. Perhaps I would rather die but why should I have to? Democracy is worth protecting, isn't it? Then, we need to rethink bringing in masses of people who do not aspire to our democratic principles. We do need to ask ourselves what will happen if the Muslim population ever becomes the majority. We need a contingency plan of strictly limiting the numbers of Muslims who immigrate to Canada and the US for our own safety and protection.

In Matthew 12: 25, Jesus said, "Every kingdom divided against itself is brought to desolation; and every city or house divided against itself shall not stand."

Bringing people into our countries who do not share our values of democracy and freedom of religions and the belief in the rights of the individual, is only asking for division and disagreement and strife and war. Our kingdoms and our cities will be divided and they won't stand. Jesus was not a liar. Unfortunately, I don't think people will wake up in time. It is politically incorrect to racial profile or to discriminate based on religion or culture. But it is these very principles of respect for the individual under democracy that are under siege. Our principles are not serving us so well under the circumstances. Democracy can only succeed if the majority of people want it to succeed. If the majority wants something else, then there's not much individuals can do about it. Except, we can act now before it's too late.

Lebanon is a cautionary tale. The same scenario of Lebanon will repeat here if we don't curtail it. What are our governments doing to curtail it? Not much that I can see. The warning, "Get out of the city. Get off the beaten trail. People will be shooting at each other in the streets," may be warning us of a massive, coordinated terrorist attack.

Whatever is coming, it will be worse than Canadians can imagine. Imagine the worst you think it can be. It will be worse than that . . . if we don't do something about it. Maybe if God's people would turn from their evil ways and would humble themselves and pray, God might hear us from heaven and forgive us and heal our land. We have walked away from the protection of God and evil is moving in to overtake us. I'm sorry to say it but in God's eyes, this is what we deserve. He has blessed us and blessed us and blessed us again and we have not been grateful. North Americans have aborted over 55 million babies. That army of people might have saved us; economically, filling jobs in society and even literally as a army but we killed off our army. If there were 55 million more people in North America, maybe we wouldn't need to bring in so many immigrants. We are collectively and individually paying a price for our sins. Get on your knees and pray, people! Trouble is on the way and your only salvation is the love, forgiveness and mercy of God. God could save all the Muslims in an instant and the future could be changed just like that.

JEWS WILL BE SLAUGHTERED

On September 4th, 2005, I received a prophetic dream. I did pray for protection and asked for guidance before falling asleep.

In the dream, I was told that "Jews will be slaughtered like lambs for the doorposts on Passover."

I interpreted this dream to possibly mean that this 'slaughter' would take place during the Passover season which is in the Spring. What better time for the Muslims to attack the Jews then during their holy time of Passover?

I also interpreted the dream to possibly mean that there will be a similar percentage of Jews slaughtered as were slaughtered for the lambs for the doorposts in ancient Egypt; one per household. If the average Jewish family is made up of four or five people, then one fourth or one fifth of the population could be slaughtered. I was not told specifically 'Israel' but I do believe it will be at least in Israel, if not other places where Jews are living as well. If it were a declaration in a Jehad against all Jews, then it would be all Jews, everywhere that would need to protect themselves.

If the Jews are going to be attacked, then this most likely means that God is not particularly happy with their behaviour at this time. This is a call for Jews to follow the directive in II Chronicles 7:14."If my people, which are called by my name, shall humble themselves, and pray, and seek my face, and turn from their wicked ways; then will I hear from heaven, and will forgive their sin, and will heal their land."

Recently, I had a vision. This was not with prayer protection as it just popped into my head so I don't have any clue as to it's reliability. I saw a vision of a news magazine like Time, Maclean's or Newsweek. On the cover, was a large mountain of rubble mixed with concrete and bits of building, etc., like after an explosion or an earthquake. People were walking up and down the piles. 'April 8th' was written on the cover. I haven't had as much success with visions coming true as prophetic dreams. This could have just been my imagination. When I saw this vision, I felt that it was of Israel after an attack.

I was not given a year that this would take place through guidance at that time in 2005. At that time, I guessed it might happen the next Spring in 2006 but it was just a guess without any guidance to back it up. With the more recent dream about four years without trouble for some people and seven years without trouble for other people including me, this may be revealing a time frame.

My new guess, and again, it's just a guess, is that Israel will be attacked some time around or after December 21, 2012. This event might take place during the Jewish Passover in the Spring of 2013. It may or may not be an actual attack by Islamic terrorists although it could be staged to look like that. If someone wanted to start a third world war, this would be a decisive way to do that. Attack Israel and the whole world would need to take sides. Canada and the US and England are allies with Israel. We could all be at war in a flash.

If this were to happen, terrorist attacks could then be ripe to take place on our homeland soils, although according to some of my other dreams, this is already being planned by terrorists. A massive, simultaneous, worldwide attack against their enemies could be organized. This could be the event that may be coming after December 21, 2015. Maybe these attacks will take place one in June and one in July. My best guess would be that terrorists would want to attack Christian countries right on Christmas day just like they might want to attack Jews during the Passover. There may be shooting in the streets in Canada, the US and the UK and around the globe. This may be the time when it would be wise to have followed the directive and "Get out of the city. Get off the beaten trail. People will be shooting at each other in the streets." If you haven't made preparations before this, you could be right in the middle of the coming 'trouble.' Although, I don't think many people are going to escape this but putting a bit of distance between yourself and the 'trouble' is usually a wise thing to do. If you can afford to move into a remote country location or have a cottage in a remote area, you might want to give this some thought. After an event like this, rural property will become very expensive.

I recently saw a vision of a Christmas tree and all the glass decorations were smashed on the ground. I think this is a prophetic vision of what is coming at Christmas time, maybe even this year, in 2012. It may be economic. There may be an event that will make this Christmas a sad time of year for a lot of people. It may be a vision representing Christmas of 2015 when terrorists attack the democratic, Christian nations of the world, in particular, Canada and the US.

Seeing that this section is of particular interest to Jews, there is something that I would really like to point out to any Jew reading this.

In Isaiah 53, God talks about His servant, the coming Messiah, and there is a description of Him found in your Torah.

The description begins in Isaiah 52: 13-15, '13 Behold, my servant shall deal prudently, he shall be exalted and extolled, and be very high. 14As many were astonied at thee; his visaged was so marred more than any man, and his form more than the sons of men: 15So shall he sprinkle many nations, the kings shall shut their mouths at him: or that which had not been told them shall they see; and that which they had not heard shall they consider.

Isaiah 53: 1-10, 1Who hath believed our report? And to whom is the arm of the Lord revealed? 2For he shall grow up before him as a tender plant, and as a root out of a dry ground: he hath not form or comeliness; and when we shall see him, there is no beauty that we should desire him, 3He is despised and rejected of men; a man of sorrows, and acquainted with grief: and we hid as it were our faces from him; he was despised, as we esteemed him not.

4Surely he hath bourne our griefs, and carried our sorrows: yet we did esteem him stricken, smitten of God, and afflicted. 5But he was wounded for our transgressions, he was bruised for our iniquities: the chastisement of our peace was upon him, and with his stripes we are healed. 6All we like sheep have gone astray; we have turned every one to his own way; and the Lord hath laid on him the iniquities of us all. 7He was oppressed, and he was afflicted, yet he opened not his mouth: he is brought as a lamb to the slaughter, and as a sheep before her shearers is dumb, so he openeth not his mouth. 8He was taken from prison and from judgement: and who shall declare his generation? For he was cut off out of the land of the living: for the transgression of my people was he stricken. 9And he made his grave with the wicked, and with the rich in his death; because he had done no violence, neither was any deceit in his mouth. 10Yet it pleased the Lord to bruise him; he hath put him to grief: when thou shalt make his soul an offering for sin, he shall see his seed, he shall prolong his days, and the pleasure of the Lord shall prosper in his hand.

This is the prediction of the coming Messiah. Ask yourself these questions, if you haven't already. When was he beaten and marred more than any man? When was he wounded for your transgressions and bruised for your iniquities? When was he brought to death like a lamb for the slaughter? When was his soul made an offering for sin? When did you despise him and reject him and when did you hide your face from him and when did you esteem him not?

This is in your Torah! I think there can be little doubt that the description here is about the death of Jesus Christ who was beaten beyond recognition and who's soul was made an offering for your sin when he was crucified on the cross. You are still waiting for the Messiah but He has already been here. Those who have ears to hear, let them hear.

Nevertheless, for those who can't hear it or accept, the next coming of Jesus Christ will be the first coming of the Messiah for the Jews. It will be the second coming of the Messiah for the Christians. We are both waiting for the same Messiah! The bible tells us that God blinded the Jews regarding Jesus so that the Gentiles, the rest of us, could be allowed salvation as well. If you were or are blind, it's not entirely your fault. It was all part of God's plan and we thank God and we thank you for it. Your blindness was/is our greatest blessing. However, it's okay for you to see clearly now, God willing.

Dear God:

"Have mercy on your chosen people, the Jews. Forgive their sins and turn away from your wrath. Place your hedge of protection around every Jew and around the borders of Israel. Cause your angels to guard the safety of Israel and to guard the safety of all Jews. Open their eyes and soften their hearts and show them in advance what the enemy has in store for them. Help them to prepare and to defend themselves. God, be their shield and their strong protection. Push back the enemy and knock him down and out on their account. Give the Jews and Israel a clear victory against their oppressors. I ask this through the power of the Holy Spirit in the name of Jesus Christ. Amen."

CANADA TO BECOME
A COMMUNIST COUNTRY

Many years ago, in the 1980s, I had a dream that Canada would become a communist country. In the dream, I was talking with a Russian leader. He told me that he was going to burn all the holy books; the bible, the Torah, the Koran, among other books. The freedoms of democracy were to be taken away. There was to be no more freedom of expression, no more free democratic votes or freedom to congregate in Canada.

In the dream, I was shown that only the Anglican Church would be allowed to remain in operation. All the other churches, synagogues and mosques were to be shut down. You could go to church only if you were already a member of that church before the switch to communism. No new members would be allowed to join the Anglican Church. If you weren't a member of the Anglican church, you couldn't go to church anymore. You couldn't even meet with others of your faith in your home without fear of severe reprisals. Except for a few brave people meeting secretly under the threat of imprisonment, organized religion was all but eliminated.

The Russian leader may or may not mean that Russia will be involved. At the time that I had this dream, Russia was a defining symbol of communism so it might not be literally interpreted. Since having that dream, I often wonder what could bring about communism in Canada. Could something like this be caused by a war with a communist country like Russia or China or could it come about after a terrorist attack?

After a wide spread terrorist attack if perpetrated by Islamic extremists, it is probable that all the mosques would be shut down. How does a government close down all the mosques of one religion in a democratic society while not closing down both the synagogues and the churches as well? It would be extremely prejudicial to shut down one religion and not the others. If the attacks were aimed at Christians and Jews, the government might surmise that the Christians and the Jews could be organizing inside of those churches and synagogues to get even with the Muslims for the death of loved ones, etc. The government might just decide it would be safer for all concerned to just stop all organized religion at least for a while and a while might turn into a more permanent solution.

There are many good, law biding Muslims. Under normal circumstances, they would wish to get along peacefully with all their neighbours. However, if a Jehad is called or a holy war is called against the infidels, then they might be coerced into joining into the killings. If they are told that they must serve Allah and kill the infidels or be considered a traitor to Allah and be killed as infidels themselves, how many would choose to die for strangers of another religion? What would you do, if you were in that situation? I think almost anyone given a choice like this would most likely choose their own religion and the safety of themselves and their loved ones. A declaration of a holy war in Canada, could be a very grave, widespread war involving a lot of Muslims with guns and bombs. There are already close to a million Muslims in Canada and this number is expected to triple within the next twenty years or so, through immigration and propagation. Muslim couples, on average, have many more children then the general non Muslim population. This same potential for an enormous Muslim army, either coerced into a Jehad or willing to participate, would be an army of great numbers in many countries of the world.

Considering all the dreams I have had related to terrorist attacks, I think this is the most likely cause to make Canada into a communist country. After the attacks, martial law and an end to our democratic rights might be the way that the government in power decides to deal with it. This may be the only way that the government would be able to stop all the fighting and control the population from re-organizing for their next attack or for retaliation and payback.

This scenario also could further explain why God didn't like the gun control bill in Canada. With unregistered guns, citizens can defend themselves. Without guns or with guns that can easily be confiscated due to a registration process that identifies who has them and how many they have, citizens could be slaughtered in a genocide or be easily taken over by military force. Canadians tend to be naive and think that because things have always been good in the past, what could possibly go wrong in good old, peaceful Canada? We live in a dangerous world with wars and disasters. Evil is all around us and within us. A lot could go very wrong in a hurry.

According to my dreams, a lot will go wrong. It's up to you whether you choose to believe any of these dreams or not. I can't claim 100% accuracy in my prophetic dreams. Some stuff comes true and some doesn't. The fact that any of it could be wrong or misinterpreted could be seen as a good reason to throw the baby out with the bathwater. But there is something to it and some of it does come true. If I'm wrong, I may have eaten some bad pizza the night before dreaming or I didn't pray and adequately protect myself from outside influences. I may have misinterpreted. I may have been working out my own problems in my subconscious in my dreams at night.

I had a dream two nights ago. I was one of eight hippopotamus and I was happy that as a hippopotamus, I could hide and stay under water for a long time. I got stuck in a hole because either it was too small or I was too big.

I racked my brains trying to figure out what the dream meant. Maybe God was trying to tell me I am too fat. I could stand to lose some weight. I'm not really sure what it means. The point is, they are just dreams but some of them do come true and some of them seem a lot more prophetic than others. Just in case any of these dreams do come true, at least some people who have read my book will have time to seek God on their own as to the validity of these dreams. They may even be able to prepare or contribute to a better future for themselves and all of us. That is my hope.

In Jeremiah 23: 28, the bible instructs, 'The prophet that hath a dream, let him tell a dream; and he that hath My word, let him speak My word faithfully.' I'm just obeying this instruction in the bible. It's up to you whether you choose to believe the messages in these dreams or not.

THE ANTI-CHRIST

A voice spoke to me in a dream and the general guidance information in and around the dream was as follows. 'People should not name their daughters 'Jennifer' anymore. The anti-Christ will do something to the Jennifers of the future. April 15th, 2005 is the beginning of the reach of the anti-Christ's reign on Earth.'

I took this to mean that people born prior to April 15th, 2005, will all be dead by the time the anti-Christ reigns. People being born from April 15th, 2005 and onward, may still be alive to be under his reign of terror. I don't know if this might help to narrow down the time frame of the rapture. The bible says that no man can know the day or hour but maybe we can know the month and the year or at least, narrow the time frame down.

It is also possible that some event took place on April 15th, 2005, that would be a catalyst to the reign of the anti-Christ. The dream could be open to other interpretations as well.

I believe the dream is predicting that a great woman of God named Jennifer will emerge during the reign of the anti-Christ. In some way, she will represent a threat to the anti-Christ and he will attempt to hunt her down and destroy her. Like King Herod attempted to kill Jesus at an early age by killing all the male children under the age of two years, the anti-Christ may send out an order against all the women with the name Jennifer. Therefore, to protect children from this future persecution, it is best not to use the name Jennifer anymore. Unless God tells you specifically to name a child Jennifer, don't do it. It's better to be safe than sorry in this case.

Some Muslims are waiting for their version of their Messiah or leader to arrive on Earth. Although I was not told this in a dream or in guidance, I personally believe that the anti-Christ will be a leader from the Muslim religion. The only religion that I am aware of that would feel justified in persecuting and killing the infidels (Jews and Christians) if they don't convert, is the Muslim religion as outlined in the Koran.

I'm sure there are many law biding, nice Muslims in the world. However, as I have pointed out before, if a Jehad were to be declared, they may unwittingly be pulled into a movement much greater than anyone's individual religious philosophy or theology. They may be given little choice but to fight or die.

I don't think that Muslims really understand how Mohammad appears to non Muslims. Most non Muslims could not comprehend following the teachings of a leader like Mohammad. He married a six year old child that was still playing with dolls. He consummated that marriage when the girl was nine years old. In our culture, this kind of act against a child is considered completely unacceptable. It's a way to end up in jail.

Some people might say that it was a different time and these things were acceptable back then. I have to point out that none of the holy men described in the bible were having sex with children. As far as we know, Jesus loved children and would never harm one hair on their heads.

In Matthew 18: 5-6, Jesus states, "5And whoso shall receive one such little child in my name receiveth me. 6 But who shall offend one of these little ones which believe in me, it were better for him that a millstone were hanged about his neck, and that he were drowned in the depth of the sea."

At first, when Mohammad was trying to win over the Jews to accept him, there were many verses in the Koran that talked about charity and being nice to your neighbours. Once the Jews outright rejected Mohammad and all that he stood for, he changed his tune from love to hate. After this point in time, we find verses in the Koran that tell Muslims to try to convert others but if they reject Mohammad and his message, then it's time to 'kill the infidels.' This is why the latter verses replace the former verses if there is a discrepancy between two verses in the Koran. Does this 'follow me or I'll kill you' theology seem a tad undemocratic, to say the least? In a democratic society, it's difficult to believe that people join the Muslim religion with their eyes wide open.

A religious leader needs to be someone that a vast majority of people can emulate. That person needs to have superior spiritual qualities that a person can aspire to attain and bring out in oneself to improve that person and improve the condition of the world in general. These leaders represent the ideal that we can try to attain even if we ourselves fall short.

Jesus was loving and forgiving and He inspired all who would follow Him to do the same. If the whole world was full of people trying to be like Jesus, loving their neighbours as they love themselves, the world would be a beautiful place, full of forgiveness and peace and healing.

Now, contrast that image to the image of Mohammad. If his followers were inspired to behave 'exactly' like he behaved towards the other people around him, it would be another world entirely. Imagine a world where young girls could not feel safe to sleep at night. Imagine a world full of billions of mini Mohammads talking and acting just like him, saying, "I'm right and everyone else is wrong. Follow me or I'll kill you." Would Mohammad's example inspire happiness, love and world peace? Would the mini Mohammads love and tolerate each other if they had different opinions or would they just end up killing each other? Every time there was a disagreement, would there be a fight to the death for supreme control?

This is what I mean when I say that Muslims don't fully comprehend how Mohammad looks to non Muslims. It's difficult for people of other religions to comprehend why people would want to follow Mohammad or emulate his personality or make him their hero to look up to.

So why do people stay in the Islamic faith? Some people arc brought up from childhood not knowing any other religion. Criticizing Islam is forbidden so people are not free to openly discuss how they feel about their religion. They may not have access to enlightening information that is forbidden to be shared. To leave the religion would most likely mean being disowned by their entire family. Most people would not like to lose their entire family so this would be a great sacrifice. Also, if anyone leaves that religion, they can be hunted down and killed just because they left that religion. That's another very good reason to stay. People in this religion who may want to leave, might not believe that they can leave without dire consequences.

There are many good Muslims with the best of intentions living peacefully in the world. It is only a minority that is the radical, terrorist element. Nevertheless, if a Jehad is called by the minority, it could end up coercing the whole group. Therefore, it would be better for them not to align themselves with a religion that has the potential to cause so much harm to themselves and to their fellow human beings. Still, it's not so easy to leave given the dire consequences they may face.

I believe it will be the anti-Christ using the Muslim religion that will eventually bring this world to it's knees and to the brink of destruction before Christ returns. Does this sound far fetched to you?

Many Muslims believe in and are waiting for 'their' saviour or messiah to come. They call him Mahdi.

Many Muslims believe their messiah will arrive on the scene once the world is on the brink of destruction. The reason he will arrive is because he loves this world so much that he will have no choice but to show himself last minute and save the planet. Some of these Muslims are not content to just wait around patiently for this brink of destruction to happen all by itself. They want to help facilitate the brink of destruction because then Madhi, their messiah, will come sooner rather than later.

The current leader of Iran, Mahmoud Ahmadinejad, is one of these Muslims. He is reportedly tied to a radical group which wants to create chaos on Earth so that Mahdi will arrive sooner. In most of his public speeches, Ahmadinejad prays that Allah will bring Mahdi sooner rather than later. He has stated that his mandate is to pave the way for the coming of the Islamic messiah. Ahmadinejad is reportedly tied to a radical Islamic group in Iran that believes that, by creating chaos in the world, they can hasten the arrival of Mahdi.

I think most people outside the Muslim world would find this very difficult to comprehend. If Mahdi is forced to return early because he loves the world and wants to save it, how happy will he be with the people who were trying to cause the eminent destruction of his precious world? My guess is, he won't be too happy with them. He might even severely punish them for jeopardizing the world he loves so much. Apparently, they really do think Mahdi is going to arrive and say, "Great job guys! Thanks so much for destroying this world I love so much!"

It is much more likely that Madhi will severely punish them for their evil deeds and they will have worked themselves out of any reward that was promised to them in the afterlife.

Yes. These people do exist and live in the real world with us. I'm sure only a small radical group of Muslims believe that they need to create chaos and destroy the world to bring Mahdi. I'm sure the vast majority of Muslims are more sensible then this. However, when someone who is advocating this is a head of state threatening to get nuclear warheads to wipe his neighbour, Israel, off the map, it's something for all of us to be concerned about. I wouldn't want to be a Muslim called upon to serve Allah in a Jehad to destroy the world so that Mahdi can come sooner and punish everyone who tried to destroying his precious world. It's a real catch 22. It's something that sensible Muslims should seriously think about before it comes to that.

Even the whole idea that God would want to have Muslims kill other people for Him, the infidels, because He is incapable of doing it Himself, is inconceivable to most people, especially North American Christians. If God wanted all those people dead, then why did He create them in the first place? And if they needed to be killed, who could kill them quicker or better than God Himself? If God wants people dead, He could certainly kill them Himself. As a matter of fact, God takes plenty of people out of this world every single day. What an insult to God to think that He's so puny and weak that He can't do it Himself and needs mere mortal men to do it for Him. It's seems ludicrous but this is exactly what some radical Muslims believe.

So many things in the Muslim world are incomprehensible to the outside world. Given their options, the best thing we can do for Muslims is to pray for them.

Dear God:

"We ask that you would soften the hearts and open the eyes of all Muslims. We pray that you would protect all Muslims who would like to leave the Muslim faith. We pray that you will guide them to a better life and to a better future. We ask you, God, to fill their hearts with the love and light and salvation of Jesus Christ. We ask you, God, to fill them with your Holy Spirit so that He can lead them into all truths, as the bible promises. We ask this through the power of the Holy Spirit in the name of Jesus Christ. Amen."

DAYS OF DARKNESS

In a prophecy that my mother received, there was mention of a time of darkness on the earth. It would be so terrifying that men's hearts would fail them. The message of the prophecy was that Christians did not need to fear because God would take care of them and this time of darkness would not last.

I think this refers literally to darkness that will cover the earth. For example, a large volcano or several large volcanos erupting at once, could literally blanket the earth with ash and block out the sun. Likewise, the detonation of one or more weapons of mass destruction could cause a cloud of ash to cover the earth.

The main thing to remember, if and when this happens, is that it won't last. If people thought the sun would be blocked out long enough for all the plants and animals and humans to die, then yes, men's hearts would fail them. But God is telling the His church, not to worry. It won't last.

END TIMES

In a dream, God showed me what was coming in the future at the end of this age. In the dream, most of the people of the Earth were destroyed. There was only a handful of people left. Everyone that was left was extremely paranoid. I was on an island that was occupied by a few survivors and most of them were army personnel. A man in a row boat was rowing towards the island. The army simply blew his boat up before determining whether he was a friend or foe. Whatever had happened in the world made them too afraid to even check him out. He was doomed from the minute they laid eyes on him and so was anyone else alive that tried to link up with other survivors. For them to be so paranoid, they must have been afraid of a bomb or that he could be carrying a disease or a virus. It was too big of a risk to trust anyone or help anyone.

As a member of this small armed group, we could have just about anything we wanted because almost everyone was dead and we could have their possessions; their vehicles and houses or whatever else of value that they had. However, the world was in a state of total chaos and destruction. The people and most of the animals and wildlife were dead. It was not an environment that anyone would be happy to find themselves alive in.

Then, God asked me in the dream to pray and ask Him to take out every person, to make sure that no one would be left alive because it would be better at that time to be dead than to be alive.

The dream was extremely depressing and I felt hopeless for months. What kind of future was this to look forward to? What was the point of anything if the world was just going to end up with nothing and no one left alive?

I kept asking God for some hope for the future. I asked Him to show what the up side was to any of this? I asked Him to show me if there was any way to stop this version of the future from happening?

Eventually, my mother brought a prophecy which partially answered my question. In the prophecy, God said that if 'Christians' would reach out to the whole world, and not just care about their own families and their own neighbourhoods and their own countries, then this future could be changed.

It was quite an epiphany. Christians will make or break the future survival of this Earth! It's up to us!

The bible states in II Chronicles 7: 14, "If my people, which are called by my name, shall humble themselves, and pray, and seek my face, and turn from their wicked ways; then will I hear from heaven, and will forgive their sin, and will heal their land."

I have learned over time that every prophetic word can have a different outcome if people pray and change their ways. There isn't any catastrophe that has been predicted or prophesied, that can't be altered or averted by people changing their actions and yes, humbling themselves and praying.

Let's not run from our responsibility for the survival of the world like Jonah. He ran from the Lord and then was swallowed up by a great whale. Let's be like the people of Nineveh who were warned by God that he was about to destroy them.

In Jonah 3: 1-10, we read, '1And the word of the Lord came to Jonah the second time, saying, 2Arise, go unto Nineveh, that great city, and preach unto it the preaching that I bid thee. 3So Jonah arose, and went unto Nineveh, according to the word of the Lord. Now Nineveh was an exceedingly great city of three days journey. 4And Jonah began to enter into the city a day's journey, and he cried, and said, Yet forty days, and Nineveh shall be overthrown.

5So the people of Nineveh believed God, and proclaimed a fast, and put on sackcloth, from the greatest of them unto the least of them. 6For word came unto the King of Nineveh, and he arose from his throne, and he laid his robe from him, and covered him with sackcloth, and sat in ashes. 7And he caused it to be proclaimed and published through Nineveh by the decree of the king and his nobles, saying, Let neither man nor beast, heard nor flock, taste anything: let them not feed, nor drink any water:

8But let man and beast be covered with sackcloth, and cry mightily unto God: yea, let them turn every one from his evil way, and from the violence that is in their hands. 9Who can tell if God will turn and repent, and turn away from his fierce anger, that we perish not? 10And God saw their works, that they turned from their evil way; and God repented of the evil, that he had said that he would do unto them; and he did it not.'

In Chapter 4, Jonah said that he knew that God was a gracious God, and merciful, slow to anger, and of great kindness and he knew that God would change his mind and not destroy Nineveh.

Can you imagine, in this day and age, a whole large city stopping everything to cover themselves in sackcloth and ashes to repent of their sins? These people were really, really evil; evil enough for God to wipe them off of the map and even these people knew that God meant business. Do people know today that God means business or do they even believe that he exists? We are an even more evil generation than this group of people because we would probably think a man like Jonah was a crazy person and fine him for loitering or lock him up.

When Jonah was on the boat in Chapter 2, and the men on the boat saw the waves and the angry sea, they knew God wasn't happy about something. Would most people in this day and age surmise that an angry, threatening sea might have anything to do with the actions of anyone on board a ship? I don't think so.

In Jonah 2: 6-10, '6So the shipmaster came to him, and said unto him, What meanst thou, O sleeper? Arise, call upon thy God, if so be that God will think upon us, that we perish not. 7And they said every one to his fellow, Come, and let us cast lots, that we may know for whose cause this evil is upon us. So they cast lots, and the lot fell upon Jonah. 8Then they said unto him, Tell us, we pray thee, for whose cause is this evil upon us: What is thine occupation? And whence cometh thou? What is thy country? and of what people art thou?

9 And he said unto them, I am a Hebrew; and I fear the Lord, the God of heaven, which hath made the sea and the dry land. 10Then the men were exceedingly afraid, and said unto him, Why hast thou done this? For the men knew that he fled from the presence of the Lord, because he had told them.

Then they asked Jonah what to do and Jonah told them to throw him into the sea. The men keep trying to save the ship but finally they threw him overboard as a last resort.

Jonah 2: 15, 'So they took up Jonah, and cast him forth into the sea: and the sea ceased from her raging. 16Then the men feared the Lord exceedingly, and offered a sacrifice unto the Lord, and made vows.

Most people today would probably not assume that a rough sea was caused by God's displeasure with someone on board. Most people today would not stop all commerce in a large city to put on sackcloths and ashes and repent just because some nut was yelling in the streets about God's imminent wrath and destruction.

Belief in God and respect for God are at an all time low when it should be at an all time high. If we could see into the spirit world, there would probably be thousand of sirens and flashing neon signs pointing to our imminent destruction but people don't seem to be paying much attention. Most people can surmise that we are heading for trouble but they don't know why or what to do about. They can't put two and two together; that God is real and He won't tolerate sin forever. In other words, the fate of Nineveh is about to become our fate if we don't change our ways.

In Revelation Chapter 20, we are told that Satan will be bound for a thousand years. Jesus will reign for a thousand years and then Satan will be allowed out of the pit again. He'll deceive the nations again. The nations, in numbers as great as the sand of the sea, will gather around Israel to destroy it but fire will come down from God out of heaven and devour them. This fire will mostly likely destroy the whole earth according to the first verse of Chapter 21. The devil will be thrown into the lake of fire again, this time forever.

At the beginning of Chapter 21, we read, '1And I saw a new heaven and a new earth: for the first heaven and the first earth were passed away; and there was no more sea.'

This sounds like the total destruction of the world to me. This is the final battle between good and evil after Christ's rule of a thousand years and it doesn't seem like much of a battle. The troops gather around Israel and God simply obliterates them. He will also obliterate the first heaven and the first earth and the sea. In other words, there will be nothing left.

I've been instructed in a dream to pray that God will leave no one alive in the end times because being alive will be much worse than being dead. Much of interpreting guidance sometimes involves guessing. I'm guessing that this total destruction of the earth that will happen after Christ's one thousand year reign, is NOT the time I have been asked to pray about. In biblical prophecy, this is already predicted and it doesn't need my prayer to make it any more likely to happen.

In Matthew 24: 21-22, we read, '21For then shall be great tribulation, such as was not since the beginning of the world to this time, no, nor ever shall be.

22 And except those days should be shortened, there should no flesh be saved; but for the elect's sake, those days shall be shortened.

I believe the time I am being asked to pray about is the time frame when the anti-Christ is ruling and Jesus returns to the earth to rule it; the time of tribulation referred to in Matthew 24. I think the situation will be so dire at that time, it would be better that no one be left alive. I believe the world will be a poisonous wasteland without safe water, without much vegetation or food; a completely toxic hostile environment. This will happen within the next 100 years(maybe sooner rather than later) extrapolating from my dream about the time frame of the rule of anti-Christ. This begs the question then, "If everyone ends up dead then who is Christ returning for and who will be alive for Him to rule over?"

In Revelations 20: we read, '1And I saw an angel come down from heaven, having the key of the bottomless pit and a great chain in his hand. 2 And he laid hold on the dragon, that old serpent, which is the devil, and Satan, and bound him a thousand years, 3 And cast him into the bottomless pit, and shut him up, and set a seal upon him, that he should deceive the nations no more, til the thousand years should be fulfilled: and after that he must be loosed a little season.

4 And I saw thrones, and they sat upon them, and judgement was given unto them: and I saw the souls of them that were beheaded for the witness of Jesus, and for the word of God, and which had not worshipped the beast, neither his image, neither had received his mark upon their foreheads, or in their hands; and they LIVED and reigned with Christ a thousand years. 5 But THE REST OF THE DEAD LIVED NOT AGAIN until the thousand years were finished. This is the first resurrection.

If the dead are going to live again after Jesus rules for a thousand years, that sounds a whole lot like reincarnation to me.

Revelations Chapter 19: 20-21, '20 And the beast was taken, and with him the false prophet that wrought miracles before him, with which he deceived them that had received the mark of the beast, and them that worshipped his image. These both were cast alive into the lake of fire burning with brimstone. 21 And the remnant were slain with the sword of him that sat upon the horse, which sword proceeded out of his mouth: and all the fowls were filled with their flesh.'

So, according to Revelations, the souls of the saints who resisted the anti-Christ, will be judges with Christ for the thousand year reign of Christ. All the other souls of the dead (and this does seem to suggest that everyone else will be dead) will not be allowed to live on earth again, until after the reign of Christ.

The thousand year reign of Christ will be like heaven on earth. Satan will be bound so there won't be any temptation or pain or suffering. I don't think there will even be any death. Jesus will heal the whole earth and the wildlife and it will be like the original intention of the garden of Eden. It will be heaven on earth.

After this thousand year period, Satan will be loosed again and the souls of 'the rest of the dead that lived not again until the thousand years were finished,' will be allowed to come onto the earth again. We don't know how long this period of time will be but it will be long enough to repopulate the earth in the billions again. We know from Revelations Chapter 20, that the army will be as the sands of the sea when they gather against Jerusalem. At this point, all life on earth will be destroyed by God.

In Revelations Chapter 21, we read, '1And I saw a new heaven and a new earth: for the first heaven and the first earth were passed away; and the there was no more sea. 2And I John saw the holy city, Jerusalem, coming down from God out of heaven, prepared as a bride adorned for her husband.

3And I heard a great voice out of heaven saying, Behold, the tabernacle of God is with men, and he will dwell with them, and they shall be his people, and God himself shall be with them, and be their God. 4And God shall wipe away all tears from their eyes; and there shall be no more death, neither sorrow, nor crying, neither shall there be any more pain, for the former things are passed away.

5 And he that sat upon the throne said, Behold, I make all things new. And he said unto me, Write; for these words are true and faithful.

6 And he said unto me, It is done. I am Alpha and Omega, the beginning and the end, I will give unto him that is athirst of the fountain of the water of life freely.

If we read further in Revelations Chapter 21, the beauty of heaven is described, having streets of translucent gold and walls and gates of gems, being constantly lit by the light of God's presence.

In the final verse of Chapter 21: 27, we read, '27And there shall in no wise enter into it any thing that defileth, neither whatsoever worketh abomination, or maketh a lie: but they that are written in the Lamb's book of life.'

This heavenly kingdom will not be a physical place where souls are trapped in human bodies. It will be a spiritual place full of spirits.

In I Corinthians 15: 50, we read, '50 Now this I say, brethren, that flesh and blood cannot inherit the kingdom of God; neither doth corruption inherit incorruption.'

Exodus 33: 20, '20And he said, Thou canst not see my face: for there shall no man see me, and live.'

The whole of heaven will be lit by the presence of God and He will be dwelling amongst the inhabitants. This would not be possible if we were still in our flesh bodies. Heaven will be inhabited by spirits.

Through symbols in their pictorial writings, we can learn a lot about the beliefs of the Mayan and the Egyptian civilizations. Both the Mayan and Egyptian civilizations believed that we originally came from the spirit world and that we gradually got trapped into physical bodies. They also believed that we will one day escape these physical limitations and return to the spirit world; to our original state of oneness.

In the flesh, we appear to be individuals. In the spirit, we are one spirit. So we will return to our eternal state of being one. In the spirit, there isn't any distance or time or separation, so we will be able to be anywhere in an instant. We will be free from the limitations of time and distance. We won't need to sleep or eat to sustain ourselves. We won't experience pain because we won't be in physical bodies to experience pain.

So if and when the whole world of people disappears off of the face of the earth, this will be a good thing. It will be a return to our original state of being. There is very little freedom in individual bodies compared to the vast universe that a spirit can travel through and experience in an instant.

The Mayan calendar that ends on December 21st, 2012, is not signally the end of the world. As a matter of fact, a new Mayan calendar was recently discovered in a cave and it depicts another 7,000 years for the world. Edgar Cayce, a famous physic of the first half of the twentieth century, predicted another 6,000 years onward from 2012.

However, I do believe the Mayan calendar has significance. I think one era of time ends on December 21, 2012, and another era of time begins after this date. I would call it a time of testing for the world. This new age will end with seven years of tribulation, the rule of the anti-Christ, and the return of Jesus as described in the bible. It is a period of grace given by God that will allow us to improve ourselves and the condition of the world. We will either succeed or fail and the outcome will seal our fate.

There is nothing that is written in stone when it comes to God and His forgiveness. We can change the outcome, but will we?

God can change His mind in an instant. God said He would destroy Nineveh. He didn't send a message for them to repent. He simply said He was going to destroy Nineveh for their evil deeds. The whole kingdom repented and wore sackcloths and ashes. When God saw that they had repented and were sorry for their actions, He decided to spare them.

In II Kings: vs 1-6, God had made up His mind that He was going to kill King Hezekiah. '1In those days was Hezekiah sick unto death. And the prophet Isaiah the son of Amoz came unto him, and said to him, Thus saith the Lord, Set thine house in order; for thou shalt die and not live. 2Then he turned his face to the wall, and prayed unto the Lord, saying, 3I beseech thee O Lord, remember now how I have walked before thee in truth and with a perfect heart, and have done that which is good in thy sight. And Hezekiah wept sore. 4And it came to pass, afore Isaiah was gone out into the middle court, that the word of the Lord came to him, saying, 5Turn again, and tell Hezekiah the captain of my people, Thus saith the Lord, the God of David thy father, I have heard thy prayer, I have seen thy tears: behold, I will heal thee: on the third day thou shalt go up unto the house of the Lord. 6And I will add unto thy days fifteen years;

and I will deliver thee and this city out of the hand of king Assyria; and I will defend this city for mine own sake, and for my servant David's sake.'

Within a few minutes, God changed His plan completely because of one prayer. There is hope for our future.

Part Two

HOW WE CAN CHANGE THE WORLD

SOLUTIONS & HOPE FOR THE FUTURE

Most Christians are longing to hear God speak to them today. They want to know what God wants them to do. They want to serve God in mind, body and spirit. They want to be in tune with His will so that they can perform His perfect will on Earth as it is in Heaven. It would be a wonderful world if Christians everywhere could line up with God's will to such an extent as to achieve this goal on an ongoing basis. Imagine millions of Christians acting Christ-like, hearing from God and obeying His will. There would be no end to the good that they could accomplish and the love and forgiveness and healing that they could unleash on an unsuspecting world. The world could be healed and saved and completely changed forever in no time at all. Most Christians dream about the day when they will meet God face to face. They long to see His loving smile and to hear Him say, "Well, done my good and faithful servant. Enter in to the riches that I have prepared for you."

The Spirit may be willing but the flesh is weak. We are on this planet to overcome the world and the flesh as Jesus overcame it. All of us have sinned and fallen short of the glory of God. We make mistakes but that doesn't mean we are defeated. Spiritual growth is a journey. It doesn't happen over night. Just like small children make mistakes and learn lessons as they mature and grow up, children of God make mistakes and learn lessons as they mature and grow up. God doesn't expect perfection overnight. He does expect us to at least try. We can ask for forgiveness if we fail. As much as we hate to disappoint God, it is our nature to make mistakes as we learn. God actually expects that we will flub up from time to time. So don't beat up on yourself too much if you get it wrong. We are baby souls and babies are allowed to make mistakes as they grow and learn. In fact, making mistakes is one of the best ways of experiencing why we shouldn't repeat our mistakes. Making mistakes can be embarrassing and painful. I made a mistake once. It was such a terrible experience that . . . well, I just never made another one. That was a joke, of course. It is important to be trying to improve ourselves though. The scriptures tell us to:

Matthew 5:48, '48Be ye therefore perfect, even as your Father which is in heaven is perfect." I don't know too many people who have arrived there yet. Jesus did it. With His help, we can get closer to the goal.

If God does speak to you, you may find it difficult to obey Him. There can be many reasons for this. You may be asked to do something that you are not yet capable of doing but you will learn skills to accomplish it and achieve it over time. You may not agree with what you are hearing. Many things that God calls good, man calls bad and vice versa. You may not like the messages you receive. For example, most of us know that God would like us to lay junk food on the sacrificial altar but not everyone has mastered the skill and discipline to avoid the junk food or to pray and fast for extended periods. Yet, we all know it is not God's will for us to be unhealthy or eat foods that have been prepared in the Devil's kitchen. Jesus clearly stated that there are evil spirits that can not be overcome or cast out without fasting and prayer. The Church is full of people with mental and physical disabilities that can't be healed except through prayer and fasting. Who will fast and pray for them to be delivered? The Devil has most Christians so dominated in the food department that we are crippled to serve God in this way. Obesity and gluttony are rampant in North America and the devil is the mastermind behind it all. If you are sick and tired and immobilized from eating bad food, you'll be plunked in front of the TV on flat on your back in bed instead of having the health and energy to be doing something great for God.

If you're having trouble believing that God still speaks to people today, consider how much the devil speaks to you. The next time you walk through a grocery store, see how many times you are tempted to buy products that are loaded with sugar, refined flours, unhealthy fats, pesticides and addictive chemicals. If you are a diabetic, good luck finding things to eat. Ditto for fast food restaurants. You already have a one in three chance of getting cancer some time in your life. The devil has laid out deadly temptations for you all along the grocery store trail and all along the road of life. The devil's voice is loud and clear. You have to be continually vigilant to out fox him.

In fact, you can't out fox him. In this world, you have two choices. You can serve God or the devil. There really isn't another choice. Every day, in every way, choose God. Whether it's a decision to buy those potato chips or not or whether it's a decision to hurt someone or help someone or not, make your decision for God and for love. The bible says that God has a still, small voice and maybe you would hear Him if you would just quit munching so loudly on those potato chips and turn the TV down or off.

You can't do it alone. Ask Jesus to help you. If you don't ask for God's help, the devil will step in because he is laying in wait for his moment to trip you up. You will end up serving one master or the other because spiritual forces are continually warring for control over you. As flesh and blood, you really don't stand much of a chance against the devil and his armies. You need God's help. You need God's words, wisdom and protection.

This book has been written to tell you some of what God is saying to Christians, as well as others today and to help you make right choices. It is up to you to decide because you do have a free will but you don't have to face the devil alone. No matter how difficult your walk in life may be as a Christian serving God, rest assured, it would be a thousand times worse if the devil was in control of you. Prisons, mental institutions and hospitals are full of people who have the devil for a master. I think the devil is the best advertising that God can get as to why we need to stay close to God. People who don't believe in God also don't believe in the devil. They are easy prey for Satan. They don't know that they can ask God for heavenly protection. Many people are influenced by Satan. Many people have their lives completely destroyed by Satan and they don't even suspect it. You need to recognize God's voice, His personality and His ways so that you won't be deceived. Hopefully, this book will help you with this. Jesus overcame the world. You can overcome the world too with the help of Jesus.

Daily Prayer:

"Heavenly Father. Have me go where You want me to go, do what You want me to do, say what You want me to say and to whom. Help me to recognize Your voice and give me the strength and wisdom to serve You only. I ask this through the power of the Holy Spirit, in the name of Jesus Christ."

BE AFRAID OF WHAT YOU WANT FOR FEAR YOU WILL GET IT: HEARING GOD'S VOICE AND OBEYING HIM

When God speaks, it usually involves some action and lessons in overcoming the world. This usually requires discipline. It's not always pleasant. Some people long for God to speak to them, but once He does, they don't like the requests He makes of them. Remember the story of Jonah in the whale? He didn't want to warn Nineveh because He believed God would just forgive them and he'd look like a fool when the destruction he was predicting didn't come true.

Remember Noah? Poor Noah lived in a time when there had never been a rain storm. He was asked to build a big boat which took 200 years to build in the middle of desert, when it had never rained. He was laughed at and ridiculed. The neighbours were sure he was crazy. It wasn't easy. Would you have obeyed God under these circumstances? It's something to contemplate, isn't it? So when you start feelings sorry for yourself because God doesn't speak to you personally, maybe you should consider that you may be getting off easier than some other people who He did speak to.

This is why the bible talks about two roads. One road in life, the easy road, is wide and well traveled. One road, the road to overcoming through discipline, is not so well traveled. Following God can be difficult. It is human nature to gravitate towards pleasure and steer away from pain or suffering and self sacrifice of any kind. It's easier and more fun in the now to just eat the bad diet than to change it. Change can be difficult.

The bible tells us that some of what God considers to be good, men consider to be bad and vice versa. We read in Isaiah 55: 8-9, '9 For my thoughts are not your thoughts, neither are your ways my ways, saith the Lord. 9For as the heavens are higher than the earth, so are my ways higher than your ways, and my thoughts than your thoughts.'

The bible states in Psalms 51: 16-17, '16 For thou desirest not sacrifice: else I would give it: thou delightest not in burnt offering. 17 The sacrifices of God are a broken spirit: a broken and a contrite heart thou wilt not despise.'

Have you ever had your heart broken? It's not much fun, is it? Sometimes what is good for your soul, is not good for your material life or for the carnal person that you are in the mortal world. Your body and mind may need to suffer so that your soul can prosper. When God asks us to obey His will, His will may not be what we want. It's His will, not ours. This can be a source of struggle and conflict. Jesus struggled with God's plan to allow him to be painfully murdered on the cross and who wouldn't have a problem with it?

Jesus knew he was about to be crucified. In Matthew 26: 39, Jesus prayed. "39Oh my Father. If it be possible, let this cup pass from me: nevertheless not as I will, but as thou wilt.

The world doesn't understand the sacrifices that Christians make. In fact, much of what Christians do, is not understood or condoned by the world. Christians offer a sacrifice of praise to God even when we don't feel like it or when our lives are not perfect. If we waited for everything to be perfect before we praised God, we'd never get around to it. The world doesn't understand how a Christian can be down and out and still praise God. It doesn't make sense to them. Christians tithe. We give away money for God's work and expect God to provide for our needs because of this. The world doesn't understand this. The world believes if you give away your money, you lose it. Christians believe that we will reap what we have sown. Christians may look foolish and gullible; even insane, to them.

If God speaks to you, it may not be a message that the world can understand. People in the world may laugh at you. Other Christians may even laugh at you. So . . . if and when God asks you to, will you build the big boat in the middle of the desert where there's never been any rain, even if it takes two hundred years to accomplish and you risk humiliation and ridicule to do it?

Once God speaks, He expects you to obey Him. There are consequences for disobeying God and I assure you, none of the consequences for disobedience are pleasant. God takes disobedience quite seriously. There is a reason why people fear God.

The bible says in Philippians 2:12, "12Wherefore, my beloved, as ye have always obeyed, not as in my presence only, but now much more in my absence, work out your own salvation with fear and trembling." If there is nothing to fear and tremble about then why this scripture?

Let's face it, no one wants to spend three days in the belly of a whale. The Israelites spent 40 years in the desert because of disobedience even though it was only approximately a two week journey to get the promised land. God can always out-wait you. He's forever but your time in this lifetime is finite. Be sure you are willing to obey Him, no matter how difficult that may be, before you start seeking God's voice. Hearing from God can be serious business. Once He speaks, He expects something in return. Your message from God may be as simple as, "Quit eating that poison!" I think it's a message that God is sending out to everyone but they don't want to hear it. The consequences for disobedience might be living with a horrible crippling disease for the rest of your life because you damaged your body or maybe you will just outright die. Don't blame God if you supported the devil's menu with your money and your mouth and now you are paying the price. Ask for forgiveness and healing and try to do better in the future.

Proverbs 23: 6-8, '6Eat thou not the bread of him that hath an evil eye, neither desire his dainty meats: 7For as he thinketh in his heart, so is he: Eat and drink, saith he to thee; but his heart is not with thee. 8The morsel which thou hath eaten thou shalt vomit up, and lose thy sweet words.'

Are you letting people who have an evil eye prepare foods for you? This scripture is telling us to not desire and eat these unhealthy foods prepared by people whose hearts are not with you. In other words, they don't care about you or your health. They may only care about the money they will make. You will get sick.

Philippians 3:18-19 states, '18For many walk, of whom I have told you often, and now tell you with weeping, that they are the enemies of the cross of Christ: 19Whose end is destruction, whose God is their belly, and whose glory is their shame, who mind earthly things.'

Is your belly your God? How can you serve both the sacrifice of the cross of Christ and the gluttony of your appetite? Something for most of us to think about. All have fallen short of the glory of God. Most of us need to work on our appetites. We need to pray and ask Jesus for help to do this.

Do you even say 'grace' or pray over your food before you eat it? I think we are living in a time when the food quality is getting so out of tune with our bodies that we really do need to pray over everything we eat and drink. Sometimes it seems like the majority of the food industry has an evil eye and they cook for Satan! Remember to pray over the food that you eat and remember to buy organic and support a healthy food supply.

THE PROTECTION OF GOD IS LIFTING

When we walk away from God's ways, we walk away from His protection. The whole world is walking away from God's ways and His laws and consequently, we are experiencing the loss of God's protection over our lives and our countries.

If we want a brighter future, we need to return to God.

The bible states in II Chronicles 7: 14, "14If my people, which are called by my name, shall humble themselves, and pray, and seek my face, and turn from their wicked ways; then will I hear from heaven, and will forgive their sin, and will heal their land."

This sounds simple enough on the surface but how do we humble ourselves, pray, seek His face and turn from our wicked ways? Turning from our wicked ways seems particularly difficult to do seeing none of us are perfect or can maintain perfection for any length of time.

Nevertheless, in Matthew 5: 48, Jesus commands us to 'Be ye therefore perfect, even as your Father which is in heaven is perfect.'

That's a tall order.

In Ephesians 2: 8-9, we read, '8For by grace are ye saved through faith; and that not of yourselves: it is a gift of God: 9 Not of works, lest any man should boast.'

From this scripture, we know that we are saved through faith and grace by asking our Saviour to forgive our sins. We didn't save ourselves. Salvation is a gift from God. Jesus died on the cross and paid the price for our sins. Even if it were possible for each or us to put in a billion hours of community service to try to pay for our sins, it wouldn't be enough good works to save us. And it wouldn't even be necessary because Jesus already paid the price. All we have to do is ask for forgiveness and we are forgiven. However, we are also expected to forgive others.

While we often hear the scripture above, we don't often hear the next verse of scripture quoted which goes on to say in Ephesians 2:10 '10We are His workmanship, created in Christ unto good works, which God hath before ordained that we should walk in them.'

So many Christians think that once you are forgiven and saved, good works don't matter anymore. A lot of Christians base this on Ephesians 2: 8-9. The scripture which follows this one suggests otherwise. We are created in Christ unto good works which God hath ORDAINED that we should walk in them. From this scripture we find out that good works are important and we are ordained by God and created in Christ to walk in them. It doesn't sound to me like we can throw out good works just because we are forgiven.

Going back to the scripture again in Philippians 2:12, we read, "12Wherefore, my beloved, as ye have always obeyed, not as in my presence only, but now much more in my absence, work out your own salvation with fear and trembling."

If salvation is already done and over once you've asked for forgiveness and you are forgiven, why would anyone need to work out their own salvation? Most Christians believe we are going straight to heaven when we die and we'll by pass all judgement too. Judgement is for the non Christians. What is there to fear and tremble about? But, this scripture tells us that there is something to fear and tremble about and it has to do with working out our own salvation.

Jesus said that whatsoever a man soweth, that shall he reap. The golden rule. We all know it. The question I have is, does the forgiveness of Christ completely wipe this out? I think of the golden rule as being written in stone. It's a law of the universe established by God. It doesn't change or bend for humans. If Jesus forgives someone and wipes out their sin from His mind, does it stop the consequences of that person's harvest that they have sown to receive? For example, you can be convicted of murder, ask Jesus to forgive you and He will forgive you. But you still murdered someone, and in the world, you can be sentenced to prison or be given the death penalty. If your sins hurt a lot of people such as robbing the elderly of their life savings, if Jesus forgives you, are those people going to also let you off the hook? There are still consequences to our actions. I think it's a universal principle of reaping what we sow. If a man doesn't really reap what he sows, then I guess that would make Jesus a liar. Does a man reap what he sows or doesn't he? How could we learn the difference between right and wrong or good and evil if there was never going to be any consequences for our actions? Could God just let us off the hook if He wanted to? Of course He could if it was good for our souls to do that. But does salvation really let us completely off the hook?

When Jesus died on the cross for our sins, was He giving us a 'get out of jail free' card like in the game of Monopoly? Was He giving us a 'Sin all you like and still go to heaven for free' card? A lot of Christians think that's exactly what Jesus did.

Many Christians believe that once you have confessed your sin to Jesus and He's forgiven you, that's it. They believe they can just sit on their duffs and wait for heaven. Not only that, many believe they can sin as much as they want to and every time they do, they can just ask Jesus for forgiveness and they are off the hook for the consequences of their actions. They love that 'Sin all you like and still go to heaven for free' card and they use it a lot. They might even tell other people about the really good news too. They tell others about this free pass to heaven and they encourage a whole bunch of other Christians to sit on their duffs while they wait for heaven.

Don't you think Jesus would be more than just a little bit upset with this whole concept? Do you really think that it was His intention to die on the cross to just let sin and evil rule this world and to let Christians off the hook in advance for every wrong doing they could possibly commit? Would Jesus really want to give Christians, or anybody for that matter, a 'Sin all you like and still go to heaven for free' card? That doesn't sound like something Jesus would be advocating when He is against sin and He wants people to stop sinning. Would Jesus really say to anybody, "Go ahead and commit any evil act against others and against me and against God and I'll just let you off the hook completely. Just ask Me for forgiveness and I'll give you a free pass to do any evil you want, any time you like."

Let's look at one more scripture to find out how Jesus really does feel about this in Matthew 7: 2123. '21Not everyone that saith unto Me, Lord, Lord, shall enter into the kingdom of heaven; but he that doeth the will of my Father which is in heaven. 22Many will say to me in that day, Lord, Lord, have we not prophesied in thy name? and in thy name have cast out devils? and in thy name done many wonderful works? 23And then will I profess to them, I never knew you: depart from me, you that work iniquity.'

Who calls Jesus, Lord, Lord? I know I do because He's my Lord. Non Christians don't call Him Lord. Who casts out devils and prophecies and does many wonderful works in Jesus' name? Not the non Christians. It's the Christians who call Jesus Lord, Lord and who do miracles in His name. What's particularly scarey about this scripture is that in most people's eyes, the spiritual giants in the Christian world, are the very ones who prophecy, cast out devils and perform miracles in Jesus name.

Matthew 7 goes on in the next four verses 24-27, to say, '24Therefore, whosoever hearth these sayings of mine, and doeth them, I will liken him unto a wise man, which built his house upon a rock; 25And the rain descended, and the floods came, and the winds blew, and beat upon that house upon a rock: and it fell not: for it was founded upon a rock.

26And every one that hearth these sayings of mine, and doeth them not, shall be liken unto a foolish man, which built his house upon the sand: And the rain descended and the floods came, and the winds blew, and beat upon that house; and it fell: and great was the fall of it.'

Do you still think you have a 'Sin all you like and still go to heaven for free' card? I think Jesus is being very clear in this scripture about the consequences of not obeying and following his commandments. Good works matter. And it certainly looks like He is talking about some very elite Christians.

In Matthew 25: 32-46, we read, '32And before Him shall be gathered all nations: and He shall separate them one from another, as a shepherd divideth His sheep from the goats: And He shall set the sheep on His right hand, but the goats on His left.

34Then shall the King say unto them on His right hand, Come ye blessed of my Father, inherit the kingdom prepared for you for the foundation of the world: 35For I was an hungred, and you gave me meat: I was thirsty, and ye gave me drink: I was a stranger and ye took me in: 36Naked and ye clothed me: I was sick and ye visited me: I was in prison, and ye came unto me.

37Then shall the righteous answer Him, saying, Lord, when saw we an hungred, and fed thee? Or thirsty, and gave thee drink? 38When saw we thee a stranger and took thee in? Or naked, and clothed thee? 39Or when saw we thee sick, or in prison and came unto thee?

40And the King shall answer and say unto them, Verily I say unto you, Innasmuch as ye have done it unto the least of these my brethren, ye have done it unto me.

41Then shall He also say unto them on the left hand, Depart from me, ye cursed, into everlasting fire, prepared for the devils and his angels. 42For I was an hungred, and ye gave me no meat: I was thirsty, and ye gave me no drink: 43I was a stranger, and ye took me not in: naked, and ye clothed me not: sick, and in prison and ye visited me not.

44Then shall they also answer Him, saying, Lord, when saw we thee hungred, or a thirst, or a stranger, or naked, or sick, or in a prison, and did not minister unto thee?

45Then He shall answer them, saying, Verily I say unto you, inasmuch as you did it not to one of the least of these, ye did it not to me. And these shall go away into everlasting punishment: but the righteous into life eternal.'

It's a long scripture but well worth the read.

He describes 'the righteous' as the people who fed Him, gave Him water, clothed Him, gave Him shelter, visited Him in prison and visited him when He was sick. If you aren't doing these things, can you consider yourself one of the righteous or do you think you appear as one of the righteous in the eyes of Jesus? They were being judged by their good works. All those who helped others were doing what He wanted them to do and those that didn't help others, were not doing what He wanted them to do. The group that did good works went on to their eternal reward. The group that didn't follow Jesus' commandment to love one another, went to their eternal punishment.

But some of you are sure none of this matters. You believe that when the judgement arrives in the after life, you'll just pull out your 'sin all you like and go straight to heaven for free' card and Jesus and the angels will smile with happiness as they usher you straight into heaven. You didn't do the things that Jesus commanded us to do. You committed every sin in the book too but none of that matters because you have the 'exemption card.' As you bypass the sheep who will be judged for their good works, you might even wave at them and think to yourself, "Those poor idiots actually tried and succeeded at obeying Jesus with the way they acted and lived their lives. If only they'd known they could have gotten away with every evil thing and have still gotten into heaven by just asking Jesus for forgiveness. They don't have the card, but I do. Na Na Na Na Na Na! They obeyed God but I'm getting into heaven just the same as them, in spite of all my evil acts. I disobeyed God and lived my life for Satan but look at me going to heaven without being judged, those stupid suckers! "Jesus. If you could just direct me to my mansion, I'll be moving right in. I think I'll take a nap while you judge the rest of those suckers . . . oh sorry Jesus. I meant to say sheep." And of course, Jesus will say, "You're forgiven. And you are right anyway. They are suckers. They could have lived their whole lives for Satan just like you and gotten away scott free if only they'd known about my forgiveness 'exemption card' policy. Because I just love it when people can sin all they want and get away with it without any consequences. That's why I died on the cross, for crying out loud." And then Jesus will say, "I'll leave you to unpack and catch a nap. I have to go now and deal with those goats, those workers of iniquity, and send them off to their eternal punishment. They weren't smart enough to pray for forgiveness every few minutes like you were, you lucky duck. We'll have to get together soon and chat about your life of evil working iniquity. It sounds fascinating. Talk to you later."

Is it just me or is there something horribly wrong with this picture? No wonder the bible says there will be weeping and the knashing of teeth. I think some people are going to be sorely disappointed when things aren't exactly the way they pictured they would be on judgement day.

Do Christians who sit on their duffs have a 'sin all you like and still go to heaven for free' card? You be the judge. But, if I were you, I would add a few things to my to do list such as: feeding and clothing the poor and visiting people who are sick or in jail. You might want to provide shelter for strangers. You might want to start demonstrating your love for others and make it a priority in your life. It's what Jesus wants you to do and what He commands you to do.

At any rate, if all the Christians sit on their duffs just waiting to go to heaven, the whole world will go to hell in a handcart. The whole world IS going to hell in a handcart and what are we going to do about it? It's up to us to change the world, to help the needy and to tell people about the salvation of Jesus. If Christians aren't going to do it, then who is going to do it? If not you, than who? Let's all get off our duffs and do something to help Jesus by helping others. When I face Jesus on the other side, I hope He will be happy with the way I lived my life. I want to hear Jesus say, "Well done, my good and faithful servant." I'm sure if you are a Christian, you feel the same way. So, let's make Him proud of us.

AM I MY BROTHER'S KEEPER? CHANGING THE WORLD THROUGH OUR RELATIONSHIPS WITH OTHERS

I believe this was the very first question ever asked of God by a man. Cain had just killed his brother, Abel, and God was asking Cain if he knew where he was. In Genesis 4: 9, Cain lied and said, '9I know not: Am I my brother's keeper?'

It's an interesting question. How responsible are we for the world around us? Are we the keepers of the planet? Can you be held accountable for another person's actions or misfortunes?

I think most people's knee jerk react would be to answer emphatically, "No way! He'll answer for his actions and I'll answer for mine."

I'm going to defend the argument that we are our brother's keepers.

Actually, all the scriptures above regarding how if we are doing it unto the least of these, then we are doing it unto Jesus, is evidence that this may well be true. Jesus certainly takes it seriously. Maybe we should too.

Maybe we should even go a step further and say that not only are we doing it unto to Jesus but we are also doing it unto ourselves. If it's really true that we reap what we sow, then we are going to get back what we do to others so we should be very careful what we do to others. The golden rule of 'doing unto others what you would like them to do unto you' takes on a deeper meaning. When you are your brother's keeper and you treat him well, then you are looking out for your own best interests by helping him and you are treating yourself well too.

When people talk about forgiveness, you often hear about how it may not even matter to the other person but you will feel better for having forgiven them. Forgiveness and letting resentment and hatred go, will help you maybe even more than forgiving that other person will help them. You will feel better when you release and let go of those poisonous thoughts and feelings.

I think many Christians get caught up in the belief in their own self importance and self righteousness. They admire themselves too much. They forget that everything they have; their money, their abilities, their health: everything is a gift from God. They are simply more blessed. Those other people are simply less fortunate. God doesn't favour Christians because they are better than everyone else. We all like to believe in our own goodness. However, having a personal relationship with Christ where you can ask for help and get it, and having the baptism of the Holy Spirit and tithing can all give you a spiritual advantage which can materialize in blessings in this world.

I heard someone once say that our attitude as Christians should be like that of beggars. We can tell the other beggars where they can get in from the cold and find shelter, protection, sustenance, forgiveness and the love of God. We are not better than the other beggars. We just got cleaned up and fed and were given shelter from the cold by God. That's something to feel very good about but not something to feel superior over others about.

Jesus said in Mathew 19: 17, "Why calleth me good? There is none good but one, that is, God."

If Jesus, the son of God, didn't even consider Himself good, what right do we have to feel self righteous and to 'Lord' it over other people? Why would Jesus say such a thing about Himself? He recognized that everything He was, was a gift from God and that He had nothing in Himself to brag about. He gave all the glory and the honour to God, the Father, and didn't take any credit for Himself because He didn't believed He was worthy of taking any credit. Jesus was trying to explain this to people but even now, over two thousand years later, some people are still getting it wrong.

Could Jesus walk around and talk and help people without God giving Him those abilities? No. Could Jesus have done miracles without God baptizing Him in the Holy Spirit? No. Jesus lived for thirty years and not one miracle was recorded until after He was baptized in the Holy Spirit. Could Jesus have overcome this world without total reliance on God, the Father? No. Could Jesus have endured the cross without the power and knowledge of the Holy Spirit? No. By lining up His life in perfect harmony with God, He was able to do what He did but only with God's help. With God, all things are possible but without Him? Everything is impossible. We are to follow Christ's example and line up our lives with God. This may take an eternity. Luckily, we are eternal beings and we do have an eternity, contrary to popular belief.

Most Christians can hardly wait to get to heaven when they die. What do they think they will be doing for the rest of eternity? Strumming on harps and singing praises to God? Yep. That's exactly what they believe all right. And there are scriptures to back that whole idea up. But, there are other scriptures too that need to be considered before we can formulate a total picture. In fact, we will probably never in this lifetime be able to completely formulate the total picture but we can at least give a try.

In John 14: 2, Jesus said, "In my Father's house are many mansions: If it were not so, I would have told you. I go to prepare a place for you."

People assume this literally means we will be living in mansions up in heaven. Of course, we will be in our spirit forms, not in our bodies, so I'm not sure a house would be necessary for spirits that can travel the distance of the universe at the speed of thought. These mansions may simply be symbolic of dwelling places prepared by Christ for us. Who says a dwelling place or a mansion can't be on another planet or in another form entirely?

In Luke 17: 20-21, we read, '20And when He was demanded of the Pharisees, when the kingdom of God should come, He answered them and said, "The kingdom of God cometh not with observation: 21Neither shall they say, Lo here! Or, lo there! For behold, the kingdom of heaven is within you."

What does this mean? Within what? Some people think it means that heaven and possibly hell too, are literally inside the hollow of planet Earth. Other people think it means that heaven and hell can be found inside of us as a state of being. The closer we get to God, the closer we get to a state of being called heaven. Being in heaven would be the same as being in the close presence of God. The further away from God that we get, the closer we get to a state of being called hell. If heaven is being in the presence of God, then hell would be the lack of being in the presence of God; in darkness. Free will allows us to move away from God's will and to make wrong choices. We can walk towards good or evil. The choice is ours. Things in the bible can have more than one level and more than one way of looking at them. Many scriptures have symbolic elements to them.

I think that most Christians believe that heaven or hell are very real places that we will go to when we die. If you are saved by Christ, you go to a place called heaven and if you are not saved by Christ, then you go to a place called hell . . . and not for just a little while, but for all eternity. Again, there are many scriptures to back this up. I tend to believe that heaven and hell are both states of being and also very real places. Even if God is everywhere, there isn't any reason why He couldn't also dwell with His people in a place called heaven. He is omnipresent so He can be everywhere at once. Hell can be a state of being and a real place too. Really bad actors who refuse to bend to God's will need to know what it's like to be in total darkness without God's presence to learn the difference between good and evil.

I don't believe that people will be locked in hell forever. If you know the love and the mercy of God, then you will know that there will always be another plan to save His children. He may not have made this apparent yet but I believe some day He will.

I Peter 3: 18-19, '18 For Christ also hath once suffered for sins, the just for the unjust, that He might bring us to God, being put to death in the flesh but quickened by the Spirit: 19By which also he went and preached unto the spirits in prison.'

Matthew 12: 40, 'For as Jonas was three days and three nights in the whale's belly; so shall the Son of man be three days and three nights in the heart of the earth.'

Ephesians 4: 9, 'Now that he ascended, what is it but that he also descended first into the lower parts of the earth?'

All of these scriptures above seem to suggest that after Jesus died, Jesus went into hell and preached to the lost souls in prison there. If there wasn't any hope for the people in hell, then why did Jesus bother to go there when He died?

In Revelations 20: 10, we read, 'And the devil that deceived them was cast into the lake of fire and brimstone, where the beast and the false prophet are, and shall be tormented day and night for ever and ever.'

The lake of fire sure sounds permanent according to this scripture. But what about this scripture?

Romans 8: 19-21, '19For the earnest expectation of the creature waiteth for the manifestation of the sons of God. 20For the creature was made subject to vanity, not willingly, but by reason of Him who hath subjected the same in hope, 21Because the creature itself also shall be delivered from the bondage of corruption into the glorious liberty of the children of God.'

The creature, or Lucifer, will also be delivered from bondage of the corruption into the glorious liberty of the children of God.

In some new versions of the bible, the word 'creature' has been changed to 'creatures' or to 'creation.' This does not make sense to me. If we look at the above scripture, we are told that the earnest expectation of the creature waiteth for the manifestation of the sons of God. If this scripture was referring to all of creation or to all creatures, then it would mean that it is the earnest expectation and hope of each and every one of those creations that they will be delivered once we are delivered. They would be earnestly waiting and hoping. How aware of spiritual things is a cat, a dog, a cow, a tiger, a mouse, a spider, a fly on the wall, a tree or a blade of grass? Are they so aware of us that they are earnestly expecting and waiting for our liberation so that they can be delivered from the bondage of corruption too? Are they aware that they were subjected to vanity, not willingly, but by reason of Him who hath subjected them in the hope that some day they would be delivered from the bondage of corruption into the glorious liberty of the children of God? Name one animal or one insect or one thing in creation that this could apply to? Even the sons of God aren't all that aware of their need for liberty from the bondage of corruption. There are plenty of people walking around who haven't got a clue about liberty from the bondage of corruption. Can a bug or a fish or some other creature be even more aware of this spiritual fact then even the sons of God themselves? I don't think so. As far as I can see, this scripture could only be referring to one creature and that's Lucifer.

In Revelations 17: vs 8, we read, '8The beast that thou sawest was, and is not; and shall ascend out of the bottomless pit and go into perdition: and they that dwell on the earth shall wonder, whose names were not written in the book of life from the foundation of the world, when they behold the beast that was (written in the book of life), and is not (written in the book of life), and yet is (written in the book of life). I have added the phrases (written in the book of life) because that's how I interpret this scripture. Lucifer's name was written in the book of life from the foundation of the world and his name is still in there. There's hope for all of us.

Lucifer's name was written in the book of life from the foundation of the world because he was an angel in heaven at that time. All of us were in heaven at that time too and our names were also written in the book of life at that time. We fell from heaven with Lucifer. Satan, Lucifer's lower nature, his dark side, is not written in the book of life and yet Lucifer is still written in the book of life. It is possible that the lower nature of Lucifer, Satan, will be cast into the lake of fire forever while His higher nature will ascend back to heaven. None of us could go back to heaven with our dark sides still a part of us either. So, our lower natures need to be burned and cast off in the lake of fire and our higher natures need to ascend back to heaven. The lake of fire may be interpreted literally or symbolically.

In Romans 14: 11, we read, 'For it is written, As I live, saith the Lord, every knee shall bow to me, and every tongue shall confess to God.'

In Isaiah 45; 23, God makes a promise to all of us. 'I have sworn by myself, the word is gone out of my mouth in righteousness, and shall not return, That unto me every knee shall bow, every tongue shall swear.'

Every knee will bow and every tongue confess that Jesus Christ is Lord. I'll bet you didn't think that this would be including Lucifer, did you? He's our enemy for now. He is the force that pushes against us that God uses for our improvement spiritually.

God has sworn an oath. It will happen. Satan and his followers may be in the lake of fire when he and they finally concede. And when Satan and his followers finally bow their knees and confess that Jesus Christ is Lord, what will happen next? The mercy of God, that's what. There will always another plan of mercy. We don't know just what that will be like because the bible only goes to a certain point in time related to our earth. There is a whole eternity of future events outside of time and space that we are not privy to at the moment. I believe that eventually, hell and the lake of fire will be done away with too if they are indeed literal places that people's spirits go to.

In John 10: 30, Jesus said, "I and my Father are one."

I Corinthians 12: 12-14, '12For as the body is one, and hath many members, and all the members of that one body, being many, are one body: so also is Christ. 13For by one Spirit are we all baptized into one body, whether we be Jews or Gentiles, whether we be bond or free; and have been all made to drink into one Spirit: 14For the body is not one member, but many.'

If we are all one in the spirit outside of these illusionary flesh bodies, can any one spirit go anywhere without all the rest? Think about that one. Can God ever be completely satisfied if any of His creations, all one with Him, are trapped in sin or in hell? There has to be a reunification at some point if we are all one and affected by everyone else.

If you really don't think God's mercy can extend to the devil, then consider this scripture.

Mark 5: 9-14, '9And he asked him, What is thy name? And he answered, saying, my name is Legion: for we are many. 10And he besought him much that he would not send them away to another country. 11Now there was there nigh unto the mountains a great herd of swine feeding. 12And all the devils besought him, saying, Send us into the swine, that we may enter into them.

13And forthwith Jesus gave them leave. And the unclean spirits went out, and entered into the swine: and the herd ran down a steep place into the sea, (they were about two thousand;) and were choked in the sea.'

Why would Jesus show any mercy to devils? Not only did He grant them their wish to not be sent to another country, but He allowed them to enter into the swine and kill two thousand of them. The cost to that farmer was enormous. Jesus had more pity on those unclean spirits then He did on living animals or on a living farmer who would lose a lot of money on this act of mercy by Jesus. Why would Jesus do that? Don't assume that God's mercy can't extend to Satan or his minions.

The heading of this chapter was, Am I my brother's keeper? I hope that I've shown you that not only are you your brother's keeper, but you and your brother are one. Whatever you do unto the least of these, you do it unto Christ and also unto yourself. If you punch your brother in the eye and you and your brother are one, you may also be the one who gets the black eye on some level. Remember, reap what you sow? There is so much connection between all of us.

I was talking earlier about the mansions that Christ is going ahead of us to prepare for us. I was saying that these mansions might be more than mere houses but that they may represent many other kinds of places to dwell. Eternity is a long time. We might live at a lot of different locations over the span of eternity.

If we are Gods, as the bible says we are, then we must be baby Gods because we are pretty far from the perfection of God at the moment. Baby Gods need to learn and grow up. I have always thought of planet earth as more of a classroom than anything else. We are here to learn, to love and be kind. We are all teachers and students at the same time.

I know that most Christians believe that when they die, they will go instantly to heaven. They believe that the non Christians will go to heaven or to hell after being judged on their good works or lack thereof. I wonder how good works can save anyone when some scriptures in the bible seem to suggest that if you don't have Christ, being the only way to heaven, you go instantly to hell no matter how good you are. It's a bit of a paradox.

THE PARADOXES OF FORGIVENESS AND JUDGEMENT IN THE BIBLE

I have struggled for quite a while with the whole concept of sacrifice for forgiveness in the bible. The sacrifice of animals to cleanse themselves of sin was used by the Jews for centuries. The idea was that an innocent animal was killed and burned as a sacrifice on an altar to God. Once God saw this animal sacrifice and the person confessed their sins and asked for forgiveness from God, God could then forgive that person of their sins.

To me, this is something similar to the idea of throwing a virgin into a volcano to appease the Gods like ancient cultures of the world used to do. Human sacrifices and animal sacrifices to the Gods seems to have been going on almost as long as there have been humans on the earth. To me, it's really a primitive concept and I'm glad that it's not the custom of the day anymore.

Here's the thing that troubles me about all of it though. I am a mere mortal human. If you commit some trespass or crime or sin against me, I can just decide to forgive you. You won't have to haul out your innocent lamb or calf, or dog or cat and sacrifice them on an altar and burn them to a crisp to appease me. For the most part, it is within the power of possibility that any human being can forgive another human being just because they decide to and they want to and they do it.

So, here's my question. Why can't God do the same thing? Why can't God just forgive a person when they ask for forgiveness without there being a whole bunch of murder, blood, death and mayhem?

I think I'll just answer my own question and say that it is logical that God can and does and did always possess the ability to just forgive sin without any creature or any person dying for it. It seems logical to me. We were created in God's image and if we've always possessed the ability to forgive each other's sins then certainly God can and does possess that ability too.

Furthermore, why should an innocent virgin or some unsuspecting innocent animal have to be punished for what somebody else did? To me, two wrongs don't make a right.

In the case of Jesus Christ dying on the cross, it's a very strange scenario indeed. Let's turn it around and imagine that you are God. People have sinned against you and they need you to forgive them. Your only solution to this is to come up with a plan to nail your own son to a cross and crucify him. Shouldn't these trespassers be the ones nailing 'their' sons to crosses? After you have killed your own son, now you can forgive everyone. Call me crazy but wouldn't it be a better solution for you to just forgive people before you go and sacrifice your son?

Why should innocent sons and virgins and animals be paying for sins they never committed? Where is the justice or fairness in that? I say, JUST FORGIVE! I believe that forgiveness was always there for the asking.

When Jesus was invited into a Pharisee's house, a woman, a known sinner, came into the house and started weeping and washing Jesus' feet with her tears and her hair and she anointed His feet with oil. She did everything that this Pharisee should have done for Jesus but didn't, because it was a custom of that day to clean the feet of visitors. As far as we know, this woman never spoke.

Jesus said this to the Pharisee.

Luke 7:47-48, '47Wherefore I say unto thee, Her sins, which are many, are forgiven; for she loved much: but to whom little is forgiven, the same loveth little.

48And He said unto her, "Thy sins are forgiven."

As far as we know, this woman never asked for forgiveness. Nevertheless, Jesus forgave her sins. Interesting, isn't it, that Jesus had the power to forgive her sins seeing that the price for the forgiveness of sins hadn't been paid on the cross yet? If Jesus could already forgive people before He died, then why did He need to die?

Jesus states in the bible that if you have seen Him, you have seen the Father because they are one.

John 5:19, 'Then answered Jesus and said unto them, Verily, verily, I say unto you, The Son can do nothing of himself, but what he seeth the Father do: for whatsoever he doeth, these also doeth the Son likewise.'

John 14: 9-10, '9Jesus saith unto him, Have I been so long time with you, and yet hast thou not known me, Philip? He that hath seen me hath seen the father, and how sayest thou then, Show us the Father? 10Believest thou not that I am in the Father, and the Father in me? The words that I speak unto you I speak not of myself: but the Father that dewellesth in me, he doeth the works.'

These scriptures indicate that if Jesus could forgive sins before He died, God, the Father could also forgive sins before Jesus died. If Jesus could do it, so could the Father.

I think I'm safe in saying that forgiveness and judgement are the opposites of each other. Assuming this is a correct assumption, then we have to wonder about some other scriptures in the bible.

John 5: 22, 'For the Father judges no man but has committed all judgement unto the Son:'

But Jesus said, in John 8:15-16, '15Ye judge after the flesh, I judge no man. 16And yet if I judge, my judgement is true: for I am not alone, but I and the Father that sent me.'

According to these two scriptures, God, the Father judges no one because He has turned all judgement over to the Son. Jesus also judges no one. So who will be doing the judging?

What else did Jesus have to say about judgement? Luke 6: 36-37, '36Be therefore merciful, as your Father also is merciful. 37Judge not, and ye shall not be judged: condemn not, and ye shall not be condemned: forgive, and ye shall be forgiven.'

In the Lord's prayer, we are instructed to ask God to, "Forgive us our trespasses, as we forgive others their trespasses."

Jesus states in Mark 11:25-26, '25And when ye stand praying, forgive, if ye have ought against any: that your Father also which is in heaven may forgive you your trespasses. 26But if you do not forgive, neither will your Father which is in heaven forgive your trespasses.'

The whole 'reap what you sow' thing seems to apply here. If you want forgiveness, then you must give it. If you don't forgive others, don't expect God to forgive you.

Now, if Jesus died on the cross for sins and all we have to do is ask God for forgiveness, then what is this scripture even doing in the bible? Forgive and you will be forgiven. Don't forgive and you won't be forgiven. This sounds a bit more complicated then what some people originally thought. We also have to pay a price or make a sacrifice for forgiveness by forgiving others.

If Jesus said that He judges no man and He preached that we should judge not lest we be judged, and He preached that if we don't forgive others, God won't forgive us, would He then die and become a judge, judging the nations and go against His own teachings?

We know from Matthew 25:32-46, that Jesus is going to separate the goats from the sheep. The sheep will be rewarded by Him for their good behaviour and they will inherit the kingdom prepared for them. The goats will be punished by being told to depart into ever lasting fire, prepared for the devil and his angels.

In these scriptures, the sheep gave food and water to the poor, gave clothes to the naked, visited the sick and visited people in prison. The goats did not do these things. Based on their treatment of other people, each group will reap what they have sown.

Is dividing sheep from goats based on their actions actually judging them? And if it is, why did Jesus say that He judges no man and why did He teach not to judge lest ye be judged? To me, the dividing of the sheep and the goats is more like tabulating accounts to see what the final balances between good and evil are. If an account shows more entries on the side of good, then you're going to heaven. If an account shows more entries on the side of evil, then you're going to hell. It seems to be based on good works or lack thereof.

In Revelations, we read that the earth is pretty much destroyed and not much is left alive just prior to Christ's return to earth and His thousand year rule. He will heal the earth. Then we read, in Revelations 20:4, 'And I saw the thrones, and they sat upon them, and judgement was given unto them: and I saw the souls of them that were beheaded for the witness of Jesus, and for the word of God, and which had not worshipped the beast, neither his image, neither had received his mark upon their foreheads, or in their hands; and they lived and reigned with Christ for a thousand years.'

Judgement was given to them but they don't seem to be doing any judging, at least not in this scripture.

After this scripture, the rest of the dead lived not again until the thousand years were finished. Then, Satan will be unleashed on the earth again. We are not told for how long but long enough for the number of people on the earth to grow to be so large that the army that comes against Israel has a number that is as the sands of the sea. God will reign down fire and destroys them all.

Then in Revelations 20: 12-13, we read, '12And I saw the dead, small and great, stand before God; and the books were opened: and another book was opened, which is the book of life: and the dead were judged out of those things which were written in the books, according to their works. 13And the sea gave up the dead which were in it; and death and hell delivered up the dead which were in them: and they were judged every man according to their works.'

Once again, what is being described as judgement here, seems more like a tabulation of accounts. If there are more entries on the good side of the books, you go to heaven. If the evil side outweighs the good side, you go to the lake of fire.

In Revelations 21: 14-15, we read, '14And death and hell were cast into the lake of fire. This is the second death. 15And whosoever was not found written in the book of life was cast into the lake of fire.'

We've already covered looking at Lucifer being written in the book of life from the foundation of the world and that people would wonder who wasn't written in the book of life if they found out that the beast was written in there. I suspect that everyone was written in the book of life from the foundation of the world.

I think the lake of fire is symbolic and represents the final purging or burning off of all evil from us. I believe our lower natures will be purged from off of us at this time and thrown into the lake of fire. Satan will no longer be tempting us. Satan, Lucifer's lower nature, will go into the lake of fire but Lucifer will ascend back to his heavenly state. We will shed our human bodies and humans will no longer exist. I believe we will return to our spirit state. We will once again be one with God, without sin.

The next chapter in Revelations, Chapter 21, talks about a new heaven and a new earth, for the first heaven and the first earth were passed away. Heaven is described in detail and there will be no more sickness, or sorrow or tears or death as the former things will have passed away. How can people be living in punishment and torture in the lake of fire for all eternity if God has completely done away with all sorrow, tears, pain and suffering? Revelations calls the lake of fire, the second death. I believe it's where our lower natures are sent to die or are burned off of us. The darkness will be purged and our true selves, as the sons of God, will be set free.

If God, the father has turned all judgement over to Jesus and Jesus judges no man, then I think that we will ultimately judge ourselves. No one can do that for us because they would reap the harvest of judgement. Judge not lest ye be judged.

Even if I am completely wrong and the hell and the lake of fire will be literally full of the spirits of people writhing in pain and anguish, I doubt that it could last for all eternity. We know that eventually, every knee will bow and every tongue confess that Jesus Christ is Lord. When that happens, what would be the point of leaving all those believers in torment? The mercy and the love of God would come into play and another plan would be revealed to save everyone. I don't believe that God is that heartless or merciless or loveless that He would punish people indefinitely. God is, by nature, merciful and loving. He is much more merciful and loving and forgiving than any of one of us and even we would have hearts big enough that we would want to free those poor souls from an eternal torment. God is much more merciful and kind than any of us.

I believe in the importance of the sacrifice of Jesus on the cross but what was it's true purpose? I believe that Jesus overcame the world and He overcame death. He bridged the gap between God and man. I believe He was perfect and sinless and that He demonstrated how a perfect life could be lived, one with the Father. I believe that every person needs the help of Jesus to also overcome this world. He is our brother and our example to follow. I believe if you pray to Him, he will help you with all your problems. I believe you can ask forgiveness from Jesus or God the Father, and you will get forgiveness . . . if you also forgive others when they trespass against you.

This is partly what I meant by forgiveness in the bible being a paradox. On the one hand, we are told that Jesus paid the price on the cross for the forgiveness of our sins. All we need to do is ask Jesus for forgiveness and we are forgiven. On the other hand, Jesus tells us clearly that God won't forgive us, if we don't forgive others. It's up to us through our good works to gain forgiveness for ourselves by forgiving others. These two ideas seem to be in conflict with one another. Perhaps both sides are right. Yes. Jesus died to pay the price for our sins but it still comes with an additional price of it being necessary for us to also forgive others. When you throw in the monkey wrench of Jesus also forgiving the sins of people who never asked for forgiveness before he had died on the cross to pay the 'price' for sin, then you just have to wonder, What's up with that? Jesus was also healing the sick before he died on the cross and before 'by his stripes, we are healed.' In fact, there are at least a couple accounts in the bible of people being healed by Jesus where Jesus told them that it was their 'faith' that made them whole.

Matthew 9:20-22, '20And behold a woman, which was diseased with an issue of blood twelve years, came behind Him, and touched the hem of His garment: 21For she said within herself, If I may but touch His garment, I shall be whole. 22But Jesus turned Him about, and when he saw her, he said, Daughter, be of good comfort; thy faith hath made thee whole. And the woman was made whole that hour.'

Jesus didn't give the credit for this woman's healing to His stripes on the cross (He hadn't died yet,) or even give the credit to the power of the Holy Spirit. He said it was her 'faith' that made her whole. Interesting, isn't it?

I don't know the complete purpose of Jesus' life and death and resurrection. I do think that forgiveness was always available from God. Jesus showed by His resurrection that we are not just flesh and blood bodies, but we are spirits in bodies and eternal spirits can never die. One very important gift that Jesus may have given us was that He broke the cycle of eternally reaping what we have sown. Maybe now, once we have learned our lessons, we no longer need to pay and pay and pay for our own karma because Christ did pay the price for our sins on the cross. Without that help, it might have taken forever for us to break free from the cycle that we are stuck in that we bring upon ourselves by our own bad behaviour. Jesus made it clear, that to be forgiven, we need to forgive. If we ask Jesus to help us to forgive others, He will help us. Maybe when everyone forgives everyone, all judgement will be done away with. The cycle of karma and reaping what we have sown will be broken and we will all be set free.

REINCARNATION IN THE BIBLE

Another paradox in the bible is in reference to reincarnation. Many people believe that Christianity and reincarnation are mutually exclusive belief systems. Actually, many of the early Christians believed in reincarnation. It wasn't until 553AD that it was banned from the Catholic Church as heresy. Up until that time, the concept of reincarnation was widely accepted in Christianity and even taught in the Catholic Church.

The idea of a man reaping what he sows as outlined in the bible by Jesus, is very similar to the idea of karma. Many religions and cultures believe in karma. It's the idea that you get back, what you give out. Even people in the world who are not particularly spiritual have a saying, 'What comes around, goes around.' This is essentially the same idea, that what you do to others will come back to you. I think that most people have some kind of understanding of this principle because it is a universal law of cause and effect. Every action has a re-action.

Many people would be surprised to learn that Jesus Himself, made some strong statements regarding His belief in reincarnation when He talked about Elijah.

In the very last two lines of the Old Testament in Malachi 4:5-6, we read, '5Behold, I will send you Elijah the prophet before the coming of the great and dreadful day of the Lord: 6And he shall turn the heart of the fathers to the children, and the heart of the children to the fathers, lest I come and smite the earth with a curse.'

This scripture is prophesying the return to the world of a man; a prophet named Elijah. Elijah was dead by the time that this prophecy was given. According to Jesus, Elijah was reincarnated into a new body as John, the Baptist.

In Matthew 11:11-15, Jesus said, 11Verily I say unto you, Among them that are born of women there hath not risen a greater than John the Baptist: notwithstanding he that is least in the kingdom of heaven is greater than he. 2And from the days of John the Baptist until now the kingdom of heaven suffereth violence, and the violent take it by force. 13For all the prophets and the law prophesied until John. 14And if ye will receive it, this is Elias, which was for to come. 15He that ears to hear, let him hear.'

Jesus said that John, the Baptist was Elijah that was prophesied to come. If Elijah had not come first, then it would have been proof to everyone that Jesus was not the true Messiah.

Everyone at that time was waiting for Elijah and then the Messiah to follow, based on biblical prophecies from the Old Testament.

When John, the Baptist, was asked who he was, he said he wasn't Elijah.

John 1:21-23, '21And they asked him, What then? Art thou Elias? And he saith, I am not. Art thou that prophet? And he answered, No. 22Then said they unto him, Who art thou? That we may give an answer to them that sent us. What sayest thou of thyself? 23He said, I am the voice of one crying in the wilderness, make straight the way of the lord, as said the prophet Esaias.'

John did not know about his previous life as Elijah. If I told you that you were the Queen of Sheba or Napoleon in a past life, would you know it to be true? Most people can't remember their past lives. Many people can't even remember what they did last week. Who are we to believe on the matter, John or Jesus? Jesus said that John, the Baptist, was Elijah. Jesus didn't say that John the Baptist was just some guy that was like Elijah or in a ministry similar to that of Elijah. Jesus said John, the Baptist, <u>was</u> Elijah.

In Matthew 17: 10-12, Jesus had this to say. '10And his disciples asked him, saying, Why then say the scribes that Elias (Elijah) must first come? 1And Jesus answered them, Elias truly shall first come, and restore all things. 12But I say unto you, That Elias is come already, and they knew him not, but have done unto him whatsover they listed. Likewise shall also the Son of man suffer of them.'

Interestingly, John, the Baptist, even wore a garment made of camel hair and a leather belt and ate locusts, the same as Elijah did. His message was the same. Elijah ordered all the prophets of Baal to be killed by the sword. Then, John, the Baptist, was killed with a sword when his head was cut off and put on a silver platter. It does sound like he could have reaped what he had sown from his previous lifetime as Elijah, if we are talking about reincarnation and karma.

The account of Nicodemus may offer some further clues about reincarnation.

John 3: 1-13, '1There was a man of the Pharisees, named Nicodemus, a ruler of Jews: 2The same came to Jesus by night, and said unto him, Rabbi, we know that thou art a teacher come from God for no man can do these miracles that thou doest, except God be with him. 3Jesus answered him and said unto him, Verily, Verily, I say unto thee, Except a man be born again, he cannot see the kingdom of God.

4Nicodemus saith unto him, How can a man be born when he is old? Can he enter the second time into his mother's womb, and be born?'

Right here, we can see that Nicodemus was interpreting what Jesus had said to mean reincarnation. The greatest communicator that ever lived was speaking to him. Was Jesus unable to communicate effectively to Nicodemus or did Nicodemus hear him right?

The next line, of course, should be of Jesus explaining that he didn't mean reincarnation. But, that's not what happened.

'5Jesus answered, Verily, verily, I say unto thee, Except a man be born of water and of the Spirit, he cannot enter into the kingdom of God. 6That which is born of flesh is flesh; and that which is born of Spirit is spirit. 7Marvel not that I said unto thee, Ye must be born again. 8 The wind bloweth where it listeth, and thou hearest the sound thereof, but canst not tell whence it cometh, and whither it goeth: So is everyone that is born of the spirit.

Jesus didn't correct Nicodemus. He didn't go into some lengthy explanation of how he wasn't talking about reincarnation. Instead, he explained that Nicodemus shouldn't marvel at him saying that a man must be born again. He explained that our spirits are just like the wind. We don't know where the wind comes from or goes to, and people also don't know where their spirits came from or are going to before or after birth.

9'Nicodemus answered and said unto him, How can these things be? 10Jesus answered and said unto him, Art thou a master of Israel, and knowest not these things?

11Verily, verily, I say unto thee, We speak that we do know, and testify that we have seen; and ye receive not our witness. 12 If I have told you earthly things, and ye believe not, how shall ye believe if I tell you of heavenly things? 13 And no man hath ascended up to heaven, but he that came down from heaven, even the son of man which is in heaven.'

Jesus also tells us about where our spirits came from before coming to earth. No one has ever gone up to heaven that didn't first come down from heaven, even Jesus.

Many Christians believe that these scriptures are simply referring to being born again when people receive the baptism of the Holy Spirit or when a person first receives Jesus as their saviour. However, I don't see the baptism of the Holy Spirit being mentioned by Jesus here. Jesus told Nicodemus that He had been speaking about 'earthly' things, not spiritual things. He asked Nicodemus, how could he expect to believe in the spiritual things that Jesus could tell him about, when he couldn't even believe in the earthly things that Jesus had just told him about, ie. a spirit being born into a body?

You can interpret this whatever way you want but I see Jesus talking about a physical rebirth of the spirit in a flesh body. Otherwise, Jesus would have corrected Nicodemus for his conclusion instead of chastising him for marvelling at it.

In Revelations 20: 5, we read, 'But the rest of the dead lived not again until the thousand years were finished. This is the first resurrection.'

If the rest of the dead live again after the thousand year reign of Christ, then this does seem to be saying that they will be reincarnated onto the planet again.

Some people argue against the idea of reincarnation by quoting this scripture.

Hebrews 9:27,' As it is appointed unto men once to die, but after this the judgement.'

Why can't this mean that you live several lives and after each life, you die, and then the judgement? Then, after the judgement, God sets up a new set of lessons for you to learn somewhere in the universe and maybe, you come back here to planet earth, to live again?

We can surmise that the disciples believed in reincarnation from this scripture.

John 9: 1-3, '1And as Jesus passed by, he saw a man which was blind from his birth.

2And the disciples asked him, saying, Master, who did sin, this man, or his parents, that he was born blind?

Now, how could the disciples ask this question unless they believed in reincarnation? How could it be the man's own fault that he was born blind? Unless you believe that a new born baby could commit a sin so great inside of his mother's womb that he deserves to be born blind, then this doesn't make much sense. The disciples had to be referring to the sins of a previous life.

Of course, Jesus hearing the horrible error of their ways, corrected them immediately and explained that reincarnation doesn't exist and that it was very evil for them to be believing this . . . however, Jesus doesn't correct them. He doesn't instruct them to believe in something other than reincarnation. He simply says the following, 3Jesus answered, Neither hath this man sinned nor his parents, but that the works of God should be made manifest in him.'

It's an answer but if His disciples were that far off track, I'm sure He would have corrected them some more. Having declared that John, the Baptist was reincarnated as Elijah, it would be a bit hypocritical of him though.

There are other scriptures that suggest reincarnation but I think we have enough here to at least open some dialogue on the topic.

Edgar Cayce, a 20th century prophet, received guidance that he claimed came from God, about his many past lives. He also was able to tell other people about their past lives. He was at least 90% accurate in his other predictions and prescriptions for the healing of illnesses, etc. Maybe he was on to something.

There have probably been hundreds of thousands of first hand accounts of young children remembering their past lives. I remember hearing about a young girl who remembered her previous life. She remembered that her husband had murdered her. Based on her past life recollections, her husband of a former lifetime was actually tried and convicted on her testimony. There are many, many similar kinds of accounts like this, if this interests you and you care to do some research.

The Dalai Lama, the spiritual leader of Tibetan Buddhism, is actually chosen based on the child's recollection of the uses of personal possessions belonging to the previous Dalai Lamas. There is a series of tests that must be passed which involves remembering past lives before the new Dalai Lama can be declared. It is firmly believed by Buddhists and others that each new Dalai Lama is the reincarnation of the previous Dalai Lamas. In other words, they believe that the same spirit has been the Dalai Lama for every incarnation of the Dalai Lama.

I have had many dreams that appear to be about my past lives. I won't go into these here but I do believe that it is possible that we can be reborn to earth again through reincarnation.

I had a dream that told me that horses could remember all of their past lives. I wouldn't be surprised if elephants also possess this ability. Perhaps many creatures do. I think our pets can also be reincarnated as the same animal. I think a cat comes back as a cat and dog comes back as a dog. Animals have spirits and they are an important part of God's creation too. If it weren't true, then why are we instructed to go into all the world and preach the gospel to all creatures? The gospel that we are to teach, is love. We can't preach and teach the love of God, if we are killing and eating the converts. Jesus said that whatever you do unto the least of these, you are doing it to Him. In my opinion, the animals are the least of these. They can't talk to let anyone know how much they are suffering. I believe that we will give an account to God for how we treated animals just the same as we will give an account for how we treated other people.

If your pet dies, it may chose to wait for you on the other side or it may come back to be with you again. That new puppy or new kitten could be a reincarnation of your previous pet. I don't think that people come back as animals or animals come back as people. I'm not an expert by any means but I think that each species would have it's own spiritual evolution.

I'm not going to go too much further with this topic. Those who have ears to hear about reincarnation, let them hear. And those who don't, don't. The main reason that I can see that a discussion of reincarnation would matter, would be if people thought it was okay to just sit around and wait for heaven without taking any personal responsibility for their actions. Knowing that you will get back what you give out, is a strong incentive to be kind to others. Thinking that you've made it and there's nothing more to do spiritually, is dangerous. I don't believe it is vitally important that people believe in reincarnation. I do believe it is vitally important that people understand that what they give out will come back to them, in one way or another. That was a very important point that Jesus was trying to make. When Jesus divides the sheep from the goats, there will be weeping and the knashing of teeth for the people who didn't help other people. Don't let that be you.

SAVING YOURSELF AND THE PLANET WITH YOUR DIET

Arguably, one of the most intelligent men to have ever lived was Albert Einstein. He stated, "Nothing will benefit human health and increase the chances of survival of life on Earth as much as the evolution to a vegetarian diet."

It takes 25 gallons of water to produce 1 lb of grain while it takes 400 gallons of water to produce 1 lb of beef. With fresh water becoming more and more a scarce commodity, it makes sense for the whole planet that we grow more grain and less beef to protect the water supplies. Also, meat production has an effect on the soil and water quality around it. Run off from cow manure and top soil depletion of lands used to graze cattle is creating a serious, growing, negative environmental impact.

The rain forests are being cleared at an alarming rate. Some statistics show that large chunks of rain forest, the size of a football field, are being cleared at a rate of one football field per second, at least that's what I read on the Happy Cow website. For the most part, this land is being cleared to raise beef. How much do we care about the rain forests? Enough to stop eating meat? How much do all those green trees contribute to our clean air? Trees make oxygen. Take away the trees, and in today's world which is constantly being polluted, how much oxygen will we have in the future? What about all the botanical treasures of planets and insects, etc. that are being exterminated along with the rainforests? Plants and insects have contributed to many of our modern medicines as well as other advancements in science and technology. Are we paving paradise to put up cattle feedlots?

It takes 7 lbs of grain or soya beans to produce 1 lb of beef but 7 lbs of grain or soya beans could feed 7 times more people than one cow. If the world became vegetarian, we could feed at least seven times more people. This could solve the world's starvation problem. How much do we care about the world's poorest people who are thirsty and starving? Do we care enough about them to stop eating meat?

I know the world's problems seem gigantic and a person might ask themselves, "What good effect could just one person's decision to become a vegetarian really have on the world? Wouldn't it just be a drop in the bucket?"

There is a theory called 'the hundredth monkey' theory. Japanese scientists observed that in one part of the world, a monkey started washing the dirt off of its sweet potatoes. This monkey taught other monkeys to do the same thing. In time, most of the younger monkeys in that group were all washing their sweet potatoes. Then, on other islands, monkeys who had not learned this behaviour by watching the first monkey, began to also wash their sweet potatoes. The theory is that if there are enough monkeys contributing to the collective conscience of the group, then that critical mass can influence other monkeys in other locations through their thoughts to do the same things. Maybe just one person becoming a vegetarian isn't going to change the whole world. But, maybe you are the equivalent in humans of the eighty-ninth monkey or maybe you are the hundredth monkey that will make that critical mass that will turn things around for the consciousness of the whole globe.

There is a great story in the movie, 'Holy Man," starring Eddie Murphy. The holy man tells a story about when he was a kid. There was a storm that washed thousands of star fish onto the beach. He saw a little girl throwing star fish back into the ocean. He asked her why she was doing that when most of them were going to die anyway. What difference did it make? The little girl said, "To that one star fish, it makes a difference."

If you become a vegetarian, it will make a difference to some animals that won't get eaten. It will make a difference if a few less acres of rain forest aren't cleared because you didn't eat meat. It will make a difference if a few more acres of grain go to feed people instead of cows. It will make a difference if a few less cows grazing don't erode the soil or pollute the water tables. When we combine our efforts as many individuals make the change, it will make an enormous difference to the world. Don't think small. Think big!

The issues facing our planet are enormous. We have to do something and part of that 'we' is 'you.' Each one of us needs to individually clean up our acts. You will answer to your maker for your actions and I will answer for mine and the whole world will suffer if we don't get it right. Do it because you believe it is the right thing to do. Educate others to do the same and maybe, eventually, enough people will see the light and we can save the planet. Otherwise, it's hopeless. We can do nothing and face the fate that certainly awaits us and the children of this planet if we do nothing. The choice is ours. I hope you will choose a brighter future for all of us. Or, maybe you think Albert Einstein was an idiot?

Here's another interesting quote. "I have from an early age abjured the use of meat, and the time will come when all men such as I will look on the murder of animals as they now look on the murder of men." Leonardo da Vinci

It has been suggested that if each person in Canada would give only $5.00 monthly to the World Wildlife Federation or to Greenpeace or to some similar organization that is dedicated to saving wildlife, then the world's wildlife would be saved. We wouldn't be having all these extinctions of species because there would be enough money to save them. Imagine if every person around the globe who could afford it, would give $5.00 monthly to save our wild planet. Endangered species would be fully protected. I'm calling on every person reading this book to give $5.00 a month for every person in your family to an organization of your choice that protects wildlife. It's not that much money. Most people spend more than this on their weekly coffee. Some people spend this much daily on their coffee. Do animals and a green, healthy planet matter to you more than your coffee or at least as much as your coffee? If the answer is yes, please send in your $5.00 and if you can afford even more, then even better. I give money monthly for the protection of wildlife. I have my donation set up to come out of my bank account automatically so I don't have to worry about it. It's all done for me. I'm doing my part and all of us need to do our part. I want a world that still has tigers in it. Think about whatever animal it is that you would like to preserve and donate to save them. If everyone would do this, the animals and wildlife on this planet would be safe and protected to the fullest possible extent.

By mistreating animals, we are reaping a harvest of mistreatment ourselves. We are reaping a harvest of polluted waters, polluted air, contaminated, depleted soil and mass starvation on a global scale. This is happening now and it will get worse if we do nothing. If we quit mistreating animals, it will have a cleansing effect on our air and soil and water and the world's poorest and most vulnerable populations will be fed. By murdering animals, we are murdering ourselves. By saving animals, we will be saving ourselves. We are reaping what we sow. So, let's sow some different seeds and reap a better harvest. Again, I recommend that every adult watch the documentary, 'Earthlings.' It's available to watch for free on Youtube. It will help you to realize how important it is that we value all life on this earth, not just human life. Jesus said that the least of these shall be greatest in the Kingdom of Heaven. Was He talking about the animals? Maybe the animals will be the greatest in the Kingdom of Heaven and rule over us for a change. Wouldn't that be justice? When God saved Noah and his family, he only saved a few humans. The vast majority of the ark was reserved for the animals and wildlife. I think this should give us an inkling as to how much God values His 'other' creatures. What would you save from your home if you only had a moment before a flood hit it? I hope it would be your pets. God would save the animals too.

In Harvey Diamond's book, 'Fit for Life,' he talks about a study of two groups of rats. One group of rats was fed a diet of raw fruit, vegetables, seeds and grains. This group of rats thrived and were extremely healthy. They got along peacefully with one another. Their offspring were all healthy. At the equivalent age of eighty years old in humans, the rats were killed and given autopsies. Their organs were still completely healthy and they showed no signs of disease.

These rats fared better than the other group of rats. The second group of rats was fed a diet similar to the typical America diet of refined sugars and refined grains, cooked foods, hamburgers, etc. They were even given vitamin supplements. This group of rats were so agitated and violent towards one another that they had to be separated to keep them from killing each other. They were not healthy and their offspring were not healthy. They developed all the diseases of modern man including heart disease and cancer. Most of them died before the experiment was over but the few remaining rats were given autopsies. They were full of all the diseases of modern civilization associated with the typical North American diet.

I hate to quote a study based on the abuse of rats, nevertheless, it's clear from this study that eating a raw diet close to what God intended may be extremely important to health. If a raw food diet could cause humans to peacefully coexist, could this potentially be the cure for mental illness, divorce, violence, crime and war, as well as disease? This is where choosing God's menu ahead of Satan's menu, comes into play. We need to give up the junk food, the addictive foods, the meats, and the white flours and refined sugars that are without nutrition and that harm our bodies. We need to cleanse our bodies through prayer and fasting. I don't think it's entirely healthy to fast with just water anymore. There are just too many toxins in our bodies and we could get very sick. Fasting on raw fruits and vegetables only for a week or two is a good way to clean out the toxins. Edgar Cayce advocated fasting by eating just raw apples for three days and then on the last night, having a tablespoon of olive oil. This might be a good thing to try to cleanse out toxins.

On Dr. Oz's television program, a guest recommended that eating a quarter cup of papaya seeds with a tablespoon of honey every day for ten days, would kill candida and all parasites and worms in the body. It's an inexpensive way to get rid of some unwanted guests and you might feel great afterwards. Apparently, most of us are host to one form of parasite or another. We should regularly cleanse out our systems and I think papaya seeds sound like a good and inexpensive way to do this.

How can we save ourselves and the world through what we eat? We've already learned some good reasons to be a vegetarian instead of a meat eater if we want to protect the animals, the rain forests and our fresh water supply and if we want to be able to feed the world's poor. Many times more people can be fed if everyone was on a vegetarian diet.

Buying organic will help to reduce the use of pesticides in the world. This will improve health for all of us as manufacturers strive to produce more organic foods to meet the demand. Coffee should be bought as organic because it is grown in other countries with whatever pesticides they want, possibly even ones banned here in Canada and the US. Apparently, Canada does not regulate what pesticides your coffee is grown with, so you need to regulate this yourself. Potatoes, apples, strawberries and other berries are heavily sprayed with chemicals so buying these particular products organically is also a good idea. Definitely buy organic sunflower seeds and sunflower seed oil, as sunflower seeds suck up poisons from the earth. In fact, they can even remove radioactivity from contaminated soil. They cleanse the soil but the residues of pesticides and even radiation that they pick up, can find their way into your body so buy these from organic growers.

For our own personal health and well being, it is important to eat as much raw food as we can and we also need to eat as many fruits and vegetables as we can. Healthy life expectancy depends on consuming large quantities of phytonutrients. Meat, dairy products, white flour and sugars do not contain phytonutrients. These can only be found in plant based foods particularly fruits and in cooked and raw vegetables but can also be found in seeds and nuts and whole grains. Cooking can destroy phytonutrients. Apparently, kale has one of the highest amounts of phytonutrients of any plant. It has about a 1000 nutrients. Just switching to kale as the lettuce in your salad a few times a week can have a positive affect on your health. When your body completely exhausts it's supply of phytonutrients, you die so you want to make sure your diet has a lot of them.

In one dream, I was told to eat 10 vegetables and fruit every day, plus another four new ones; presumably trying new types on a constant basis. If you have one meal that's a salad with all kinds of different varieties of vegetables, you can get quite a variety. If another meal is predominately different kinds of fruit, then you will be able to get lots of fruit into your body. I like making salads. I make fruit smoothies in my vitamix. I try to eat both vegetables and fruit regularly. I still have moments when I give in to junk food but we can only do our best. I'm getting better. Dr. Mark Hyman, author of the book, 'The Blood Sugar Solution,' says that the two worst things we consume for the health of our bodies, are milk and gluten. I feel much better and I have a sharper mind when I eat gluten free. This might work for you too.

Milk can be carcinogenic when consumed in large quantities. In fact, milk was added to the original recipe for the porridge that was given to starving people overseas. Some of the children developed liver cancer. When the milk protein was cut back, the children no longer developed the disease. We are the only mammals that drink milk after weaning. It's just not natural to keep consuming it into adulthood and we aren't even drinking human milk. We are drinking cow's milk, designed to fatten up baby cows that can grow to literally weigh a ton. Furthermore, when cow's milk is heated or pasteurised and then fed back to a calf, the calf can die. Apparently, raw milk is the only healthy cow's milk for a cow. So, I recommend that if you are a baby cow, you should drink it raw. Otherwise, it's most likely not the best for you.

If you eat healthy, your body and brain will work better. You might even feel so good that you feel like exercising. You might even feel good enough to go for a walk. If you eat junk food, especially salty snacks like potato chips, you may feel lethargic and you might find yourself sitting in front of the TV feeling that you have no energy. How can you live your life for yourself or for God or for others if you are passed out in front of the TV all day? One of Satan's greatest tricks is getting people to eat bad food and then keeping them immobile as a result. He knows you can't do much good in the world if he has you down and out physically. Don't let him win. Eat better and screen what you watch on TV. Limit your hours of TV. You can't serve TV or your stomach and God too. Who is your master when it comes to food and the TV? If it isn't God, then you need to pray for deliverance from this slavery of Satan. God created you for greater things.

So many people are sick and unhealthy and their diets may be completely to blame. They go to medical doctors, who can often offer them a diagnosis but not necessarily give them a cure. In emergency situations, doctors can sometimes be invaluable. However, most medical doctors receive a lot of hours of training to know the different pharmaceutical drugs to give to people for different conditions, but very few hours learning about how nutrition and natural supplements affect the health of their patients. It is a sad state of affairs when doctors can kill more patients then the top three killers of heart disease, stroke and cancer. Doctors kill approximately 15 million people a year on a worldwide basis. If it was any other profession, they would go to jail for malpractice or manslaughter. Most of these deaths can be attributed to the side effects of pharmaceutical drugs that doctors prescribe to their patients. Have you ever seen those commercials? It's difficult to believe that anyone would still go ahead and take many of these drugs knowing the side effects in advance of actually experiencing them. And yet, the Medical Association is so powerful that no natural ingredient or herb can be attributed with healing any condition. Millions of people die yearly due to doctor error but if one person even gets slightly ill from a natural remedy, it is pulled from the shelves like it was brewed by Satan himself. Everyone must protect themselves from lawsuits by telling their readers, like I am forced to tell you now, that you must consult a medical doctor's opinion before doing anything that I have to say that might improve your health. Contrary to popular belief, doctors do not know everything there is to know regarding your health but they do have a very powerful medical association behind them.

In an article by Dr. Barbara Starfield, which was published in the Institute of Medicine report, doctors are cited as the third leading cause of death in the United States. It was later published in the Journal of the American Medical Association, JAMA, which has the largest circulation of any medical journal on the globe. This article spelled out the approximate number of deaths per year in the US from doctors making mistakes. There were approximately 12,000 deaths from unnecessary surgery, 7,000 deaths from medical errors in hospitals, 20,000 deaths from other errors in hospitals, 80,000 from infections in hospitals and 106,000 from doctor prescribed drugs. Doctors kill approximately 225,000 people in the US in one year alone.

So, if you thought trusting your doctor was your best course of action, you may want to rethink that. You may have a greater chance of dying from what your doctor does to you or prescribes for you, than you have of dying from your illness.

While doctors can be very helpful in emergency situations and for diagnosing disease, they are usually not educated thoroughly on the latest natural treatments or on the nutritional effects of food on human health. There are many great alternative options available without the same side effects as pharmaceutical drugs. Once again, I must warn you, that you shouldn't use any of them without first consulting your medical doctor. No one is allowed to claim that any natural supplement or food can heal you or treat your disease so, I guess this next part is for entertainment purposes.

Vitamin D, omega 3, aged garlic, echinacea, ginseng, among many other natural supplements, can be investigated on the internet for their contribution to the improvement of health. If you are a vegetarian, it may interest you that white chia seeds apparently have eight times more omega 3 than salmon. My favourite natural supplement is GSE or grapefruit seed extract. It acts as a natural antibiotic.

Many bacteria have become resistant to antibiotics. These super bugs can be life threatening because they may not respond well to traditional medical treatments. GSE can kill some forms of these super bugs.

I know of a person who was diagnosed with gangrene in his finger. The antibiotics were not working. The doctor was going to amputate his finger within a couple of days if things didn't improve. His finger was completely black. A combination of soaking the finger in a solution of Dettol (a powerful disinfectant) and water, as well as heavy doses of GSE, resulted in the finger beginning to turn pink within that couple of days. The doctor decided not to amputate his finger.

I had a very bad cold. I took GSE drops in hot tea and within one hour, my cold was completely gone. On other occasions, my cold symptoms did not go away so quickly or dramatically. However, GSE always seems to help. Antibiotics kill both the good and the bad bacteria. GSE only kills the bad bacteria. It is kinder to the good bacteria and the probiotics in your digestive tract. It's my first choice before consenting to antibiotics.

In fact, I have a personal prejudice against antibiotics. I had sinusitis every Spring and Fall for a few years and I had to be treated each time with antibiotics. Each time it reoccurred, it was much worse than the last time. I could look down the road and see the future. Eventually, this thing could get pretty bad and even kill me. Apparently, you can die from it. I wanted to change directions. The medical profession had offered me their solution and it wasn't working for me.

The next time I had sinusitis, I turned to homeopathic supplements. It was a real battle the first time I tried this. However, I did recover. The next time I had sinusitis, it was less severe. Each successive time I had returning bouts, they were less and less severe as I treated the condition with homeopathic supplements. Eventually, my sinusitis went away forever. I haven't had it now for years. I credit my 'cure' with using homeopathy. The medical profession didn't have a cure for me. In fact, if I'd gone that route, I might not be here now. I might have become one of the statistics of those 15 million people killed annually by their doctors. I'm not saying GSE will help you or cure you of anything. I'm only saying it really helped me and you can take from that whatever you like. You might want to consult your doctor before trying it.

At any rate, eating healthy is a great idea. Imagine a world where the Christians were all so healthy that they had the energy to make money and to help others. Imagine if everyone ate organic and was vegetarian. The world's poor might finally get enough to eat once we lay down our addictions and our gluttony on God's altar of sacrifice. A lot of pollution would be eliminated, both in our bodies and in our world. The world would change completely if we could only find the strength to change. Ask God for help through the power of the Holy Spirit in the name of Jesus.

Dear God:

"Please deliver us from gluttony, obesity and from the addictions to foods. Help us make it through the restaurants and the grocery store aisles without giving in to temptation. Help us to crave foods that are healthy for us. Help us to put the needs of others ahead of our own selfish desires. We ask this through the power of the Holy Spirit in Jesus' name. Amen."

CHANGING THE WORLD THROUGH PRAYER, MEDITATION AND PRAISE

The Black Bird Dream and the Importance of Praise:

A few years ago, I had a dream about a giant black bird. I think it was a raven. The bird was very tall, maybe 6 feet tall or more. It was perched in a window sill and was looking at me through the glass from the outside of the building. I was aware that it was aware of me and vice versa. I was aware that it was coming to destroy my family. I was told in the dream that the only way that this bird could be defeated was through praising God.

Subsequently, I had another dream that my family was at a log cabin in the country. The bird was circling in the sky outside. We knew if we went outside, it would get us. It was so big, it could have just picked us up and carried us away.

After having these dreams, I was curious if God had been speaking to anyone else about this bird. I didn't find anything for a few years. Then, recently, I found a website hosted by two prophetic dreamers, Dumitru Duduman and Michael Boldia at Hands of Help Ministries. A similar dream has been posted there about a giant black bird. In a dream, it was explained that this bird (demon) has been given authority to attack the true Christians who serve God with their whole beings and not just with their words.

In Thessalonians 5: 16-18, we are instructed to, '16Rejoice evermore. 17Pray without ceasing. 18In everything give thanks: for this is the will of God in Christ Jesus concerning you.'

Psalms 22: 3 states, 'But thou art holy, O thou, that inhabitest the praises of Israel.'

Not only is it the will of God that you pray endlessly and give thanks in everything, but we are told that God dwells in the praises of His people. The more you praise God, the closer God gets to you. The more you grumble, the more He departs. Do you want God to be close to you? Then pray and praise. If you want Satan to shimmy up to you, grumble til your heart's content.

Praise is powerful. The only way to defeat this powerful bird is to praise God in all circumstances. I know this is easier said than done but let's at least give it a try, shall we? If there ever was a place that the devil has most of us bound, it's in our grumbling against God. Unpleasant and cruel things happen to us and we blame God for allowing these things to happen to us. Even though I know that a life without problems doesn't exist, I admit it, I'm a grumbler. I have to struggle to praise God. The bible calls it 'the sacrifice of praise' and it can feel like a giant sacrifice to praise God, not just for the good things in life and the blessings, but especially for the bad things too.

I had just read the book, 'Prison to Praise,' by Merlin R. Carothers. If you haven't read the book, I recommend that you do. It's an oldie but a goodie.

I was driving in to the city of Ottawa from out in the country where I lived at the time. I wasn't all that sure about the roads and the street signs, being a young and inexperienced driver. I followed a city bus because I figured if he could turn at the intersection, then it was alright for me to turn too. As soon as I turned the corner, I could see the error of my ways. Several cars, including mine, were being directed to a side street by a police officer. I could see the officer coming towards me, giving tickets to every driver in the cars ahead of me as he got closer. I knew there was no way out. I was going to get a ticket and that was that. I already knew I didn't have the money to pay for the ticket. I remembered the book, Prison to Praise, and decided to praise God for the situation. What a horrible feeling of surrender and defeat as I squirmed to praise God in spite of my pride for what seemed like a horrible tragedy to me. It was a humbling, helpless feeling.

I braced myself for the inevitable when the officer reached my car and asked me for my driver's licence. He asked me if I had been aware that there were no left turns allowed at the intersection. I explained that I was from out of town and that I had followed the bus because I figured that the bus driver would know how to drive being a professional. He explained to me that buses were allowed to turn at that intersection but not other cars. I said I didn't realize that there was one set of rules for the buses and another set of rules for other people. Suddenly, the police officer returned my driver's licence and said he was just giving me a warning this time and to see that I didn't do it again. I could barely believe it! All those other cars got tickets but I didn't. Praising God had worked a miracle as far as I was concerned.

My whole life I have struggled to praise God. I think I'm a natural born complainer. This is not a good trait for a Christian to have. I have excused myself in the past by saying, "If other people had to live my life and go through all the trials and tribulations that I've had to go through, they'd be complainers too." Of course, everyone has trials and tribulations and the more of those that you have, the more you need to praise God and pray for help. Then you get to that one person or problem that you just can't bring yourself to praise God for . . . it's difficult to do, that's for certain.

The Israelites complained against God too. They were in the desert for forty years even though their destination was only about a two week journey. I wonder how fast they would have gotten there if they had just praised God. Do you want to spend forty years in disagreement with God or would you rather just get it over with quickly? Accept the situations He brings your way and praise God for them. There must a lesson in it that is good for your soul, or else you wouldn't need to go through it and God wouldn't be allowing it to happen to you.

Don't forget that Satan had to ask permission from God before he could do anything to Job and God gave His permission to Satan to let him test him.

Job 1: 8-12, 8'And the Lord said unto Satan, hast thou considered my servant Job, that there is none like him in the earth, a perfect and an upright man, one that feareth God, and escheweth evil?

9Then Satan answered the Lord and said, Doth Job fear God for nought? 10 Hast not thou made an hedge about him, and about his house, and about all that he hath on every side? Thou hast blessed the work of his hands, and his substance is increased in the land.

11But put forth thine hand now, and touch all that he hath, and he will curse thee to thy face. 12And the Lord said unto Satan, Behold, all that he hath is in thy power; only upon himself put not forth thine hand. So Satan went forth from the presence of the Lord.'

This scripture shows us that nothing bad can happen in our lives without God allowing it. Satan can't touch us without God's permission. In the Lord's prayer, we are instructed to pray and ask God daily to, 'Lead us not into temptation but deliver us from evil.' Asking for this protection from evil, declares to God that we recognize His authority over our lives and even that we recognize His complete control over Satan and evil in our lives. Satan is our enemy for now. He is the force that pushes against us to force us to grow and learn. Without an enemy, we might just sit like jelly getting no where at all spiritually. If Satan's only purpose was to show us what the opposite of God's light and love looks like, then that would be a good thing for us to learn. We must praise God for both the good and the bad things that happen to us. Through praise, we are telling God that we trust His judgement. We demonstrate our faith through praise that God knows what He is doing in our lives, even if we can't understand the bad things that happen. All things can work together for good for those who love the Lord. Praise releases the power of God into any situation.

In Merlin Carothers' book, 'The Power in Praise,' there are many examples of praise resulting in miracles. A man and his wife prayed for thirty years for the salvation of the husband's drunken father. After one night of sincere praise, the father visited and they were able to witness to him about Jesus. Within a few weeks, he was saved and delivered from alcohol. There are many similar examples that can be found in Carothers' numerous books.

If you are a sincere Christian, a black bird may be coming to attack your family too and the only protection for all of you may be found in praising God. If you want God to get closer to you and come up with solutions to your problems, thank Him for everything. Praise attracts the presence and the power and the love of God and who couldn't use some more of that.

THE SALVATION OF JESUS CHRIST

I believe that every person needs to turn their life over to a higher authority. We are mere mortals. We can't fight the dark principalities and powers of the spiritual realm all by ourselves. We are simply no match for the power of evil. It is only through our allegiance to the authority of good, that we can triumph over evil and be protected. I think this is not a coincidence. God wants us to move closer to Him. Satan drives us closer to God.

This is, once again, where the New Age movement fails to fully recognize the need for God in our lives. They tell us that we are God and therefore we can do it all by ourselves and we don't need God to help us. This is the same mistake that Lucifer made when he fell from heaven. He thought he was equal to God and found out that he wasn't. He paid a terrible price for his vanity. Let's not keep making the same mistake.

God, the Father, is higher and greater than all. We can't do anything without Him. He is the glue that holds us together. He is the glue that holds the universe together. You can't get rid of Him. You can't survive without him. You can't succeed without Him. If you ever think you did, you were deluded. You can't lift one finger without Him or search one brain cell for information without Him. We all need God. We were made for Him and by Him. Our purpose for existing is ultimately to be companions to Him and for Him to be a companion to us.

There are numerous books written on the purposes of Jesus' life and death. I recommend you read up on the topic. The topic is too vast to fully investigate in this book. I am just interjecting food for thought regarding our deeply held beliefs and how some of what we believe needs to be expounded upon. The mysteries of God and Jesus will most likely never be fully understood in this lifetime. I can't begin to cover it all here.

Please understand that I am not trying to minimize what Jesus did. I'm just pointing out that there is more to all of it. There is more to forgiveness then just being forgiven by God or Jesus. We must also forgive others or the heavenly Father will not forgive us. Jesus said we had to forgive others to be forgiven, and we can't call Him a liar, now can we? I have questions about how forgiveness was given before Jesus had died. We are created in the image of God.

Humans have always had the ability to forgive one another. It stands to reason that God also always had the power to forgive us without some poor innocent creature or son of God having to die for it. I could be completely wrong but I don't think so. I have questions about how healings could take place before Christ's stripes could heal us. My point is that there is more to this picture than meets the eye.

God did send Jesus to Earth. Jesus did die on the cross for a purpose. He did overcome this world. He did overcome death. He is our big brother. He is our example of how to live our lives. He did bridge the gap between God and man. He did make an atonement for our sins, although in some ways that I can't fully comprehend. He is someone that we can turn to when we have problems. When no one else wants to hear about it, He does. When no one else can help you with it, He can. I believe every person needs to ask Jesus Christ into their heart to rule there. Someone is going to rule there and your choice is Jesus or Satan. You get to choose. Every day in every way, choose Jesus. When Satan tells you to eat junk food or presents you with some other temptation, resist and he will flee from you. Ask Jesus to help you to resist because on your own, this will be next to impossible in some instances. So, if you haven't turned you life over to the control and direction of Jesus Christ, I urge you to do it now. You need Him . . . . and He needs you too. If you love someone, you need them and Jesus loves you. Just ask Jesus to come into your heart and reign there. Ask Him to be your friend and to help you with your problems, and He will. He has been waiting for you to ask.

In John 14:6, Jesus said, "I am the way, the truth and the life: no man cometh unto the Father, but by me." Don't dismiss Jesus Christ, God's Holy Emissary. I believe we all desperately need Him. I do consider Jesus the centre off my spiritual life and you should make Him the centre of your spiritual life too. You can't get to a much higher spiritual state than where Jesus is. If we hang around Him, maybe some of that higher state of being and divine intelligence will rub off onto us.

Dear Jesus:

I believe that you love me and that you died on the cross for me. I surrender my life and my will to you. I invite you into my heart and into my life to be my Lord and saviour. I ask you to forgive my sins as I forgive others their sins against me. Please help me with all of my problems. I ask this through the power of the Holy Spirit in your name, Jesus.

THE BAPTISM OF THE HOLY SPIRIT

One extremely important thing that Jesus did for us was that He brought the full presence and the power of the Holy Spirit to Earth. Before Jesus, there were isolated incidences of healing and manifestations of the power of God. In fact, ropes were tied around the high priests who entered into God's holy temple. Some of them died when they entered into the presence of God and then other people could pull their dead bodies back out with the ropes that had been attached to them. You couldn't be around the presence and power of God unless you were a very holy person and even then, look out.

For thirty years, Jesus did not perform any miracles or manifest much in the way of the supernatural power of God. It wasn't until Jesus was baptized in water by John, the Baptist, that the Holy Spirit descended on Him in the form of a dove. After this experience, Jesus began His miracle working ministry.

In John 16:7, Jesus said, "Nevertheless I tell you the truth; It is expedient for you that I go away: for if I go not away, the Comforter will not come unto you; but if I depart, I will send him unto you."

In John 15: 26, Jesus said, "But when the Comforter is come, whom I will send unto you from the Father, even the Spirit of truth, which proceedeth from the Father, he shall testify of me."

In John 14: 26, Jesus said, "But the Comforter, which is the Holy Ghost, whom the Father will send in my name, he shall teach you all things, and bring all things to your remembrance, whatsoever I have said unto you."

In Acts 2: 1-4, we read, '1And when the day of Pentecost was fully come, they were all with one accord in one place. 2And suddenly there came a sound from heaven as of a rushing mighty wind, and it filled all the house where they were sitting. 3And there appeared unto them cloven tongues like as of fire, and it sat upon each of them. 4And they were all filled with the Holy Ghost and began to speak with other tongues, as the Spirit gave them utterance.'

This created such a noise that other men outside came in and each of them heard the disciples speaking in foreign tongues and each of them understood what they were saying in their own language. They knew that the disciples were all Galilaeans and that they couldn't speak in other languages. They were speaking through the power of the Holy Ghost.

These men thought that the disciples were drunk but Peter corrected them.

In Act 2: 15-18, Peter said, '15For these are not drunken, as ye suppose, seeing it is but the third hour of the day. 16But this is that which was spoken by the prophet Joel; 17 And it shall come to pass in the last days, saith God, I will pour out my Spirit upon all flesh: and your sons and your daughters shall prophesy, and your young men shall see visions, and your old men will dream dreams: 18And on my servants and on my handmaidens I will pour out in those days my Spirit; and they shall prophecy.'

We hear more about some of the gifts of the Spirit in I Corinthians 12: 6-11.

'6 And there are diversities of operations, but it is the same God which worketh all in all. 7But the manifestation of the Spirit is given to every man to profit withal. 8For to one is given by the Spirit the word of wisdom; to another the word of knowledge by the same Spirit; 9To another faith by the same Spirit; to another the gifts of healing by the same Spirit; 10To another the working of miracles; to another prophecy; to another discerning of spirits; to another divers kinds of tongues; to another the interpretation of tongues: 11But all these worketh that one and the sameself Spirit, dividing to every man severally as He will.'

There are, no doubt, many more gifts of the Spirit. These gifts are available to each and every one of us now that Jesus sent the Holy Spirit to us.

If you have not been baptized in the Holy Spirit, it's time that you were. Without the Holy Spirit, even Jesus could not have performed miracles. The baptism of the Holy Spirit was the secret of His great miracle working success.

The Holy Spirit will teach you and lead you into all truths. You may get many gifts from the Spirit. You may speak in another spiritual language or even speak in a language spoken on earth right now. You might get the gift of prophecy. You might receive the gift of healing so that when you pray for people, the Holy Spirit will heal them in Jesus' name. The power of God can be released in your life.

I highly recommend that if you want this experience, that you seek out others to pray for you, that have already been baptized in the Holy Spirit. Their faith and prayers and the atmosphere of praise and worship that draws the presence and the power of the Holy Spirit, will have a powerful impact on your experience.

However, it is not necessary that you have other people to assist you. You can ask God right now to fill you with His Holy Spirit. I suggest you spend an hour praising and worshipping God first. You can do this by listening to anointed Christian music. If you don't know the difference between anointed and not anointed music, then you may need some assistance to find the right music. Then, once you have drawn in the presence of God, and by that I mean, God dwells in the praises of His people, then you can ask God to fill you with His Holy Spirit.

I should tell you that some people feel absolutely nothing at this point. I have heard of people suddenly waking up in the night to find themselves praying in a foreign language or tongue. The workings of the Holy Spirit will continue gradually as we mature spiritually throughout our lives. If the Holy Spirit just suddenly changed everything about you, the shock would probably be too great for a person to withstand. He stands by you throughout your life, leading you into all truths and explaining the mysteries of God to you. It takes time for everyone so be patient.

Some people have a big experience. You may have seen videos of people rolling around on the floor or roaring like lions in a religious service and you may have thought they were all nuts. Sometimes, when the Holy Spirit comes into a person, that person may have a lot of inner darkness and oppression. They can even have a demon or a demonic stronghold in their lives. The devil does not easily give up his strongholds over people. When the presence and the power of the Holy Spirit comes in contact with that darkness, it can be a struggle between the light and the darkness or between good verses evil. The high vibration of the Spirit of God meets with the low vibration of the spirit of man and the spirit of devils. The effect can be dramatic. It will most certainly be cleansing for the person it happens to but it may be a humbling experience.

We cannot change the world for God without the presence and the power of God. We need as many people as possible to switch allegiance from the darkness to the light. This can be done very effectively by getting as many people as possible to receive Jesus as their saviour and to receive the baptism of the Holy Spirit to drive out the darkness in each human soul. Many people don't even realize that they are under the control of Satan. They don't know that they are being deceived. Many things look like the right thing to do, but without the discernment of the Holy Spirit, you can think you are doing the right thing when you may be doing exactly the wrong thing.

When Jesus died on the cross, He prayed a simple prayer for his murderers. "Forgive them Father, for they know not what they do."

Those people probably believed they were doing God a favour by killing off this blasphemer named Jesus. In John 16:2, the bible says that the time will come when some Christians will be persecuted and even killed by people who think they are doing God a service. Radical Muslims may fall into this category. Until the blind fold is removed from their eyes, they don't know any better. This is why the baptism of the Holy Spirit is so important. Those people who are being deceived will eventually be led into all truths by the Holy Spirit, and at that point, the devil won't be able to deceive them anymore.

It is vital to the salvation of the world that as many people are baptized in the Holy Spirit as possible. Without God's Holy Spirit working in them, they may be nice, well meaning people but they can be completely deceived into thinking that what is wrong is right, and what is right, is wrong. They are sitting ducks and they can become pawns in the hands of Satan and not even have a clue that this is what is going on.

There are many, many books on the baptism of the Holy Spirit and on the presence and the power of the Holy Spirit. Get some good books on the topic and read them. My book would never have an ending if I went into every detail of every topic I'm bringing forward here. So, if you are interested in the workings of the Holy Spirit (and I sincerely hope you are) then read more on the topic.

It is important to note that with both accepting Jesus as the Lord of your life and receiving the baptism of the Holy Spirit into your life, this can and will bring the presence of angels into your life. Angels, is another whole giant topic and I would urge you to read further on this topic as well. They are the invisible soldiers of God while we are the visible soldiers of God.

If we want to change this world, then we must first change ourselves. A house is only as clean and neat as the people who live in it. A house is only as loving and peaceful as the people who live in it. A house is only as holy as the people who live in it. Our world will only be as heavenly as the people who live in it. To save this planet, we must raise our own spiritual vibrations and the spiritual vibrations of the people around us. Accepting Jesus as your saviour and asking for the presence and power of God to come into your life through the Holy Spirit, are two great places to begin when trying to raise our spiritual vibrations. Just like eating vibrant, raw, health promoting foods raises the health of your body, so does the presence of Jesus and the Holy Spirit improve your spiritual health. If enough people get healthy, we can heal the planet. Heaven on earth can be achieved when the vast majority of people of earth become heavenly. Start with yourself and then branch out. Each time a life light gets brighter, the whole world is affected. If enough of us shine our bright light out into the darkness, then the whole earth can be clothed in the light of God.

In Acts 2: 17, quoted above, we learn that it is the intention of God, in the last days, to pour out His spirit upon <u>ALL</u> flesh. Let's join in with the purpose of God and begin and continue the process. The salvation of the world depends on this.

Dear God:

"Please forgive me for all of my sins, as I forgive others who have sinned against me. I am willing to be a vessel for the Holy Spirit to work through on this earth, to help myself as well as others. Please fill me with your precious Holy Spirit so that He can clean all darkness out of me and lead me into all truths. Give me the gift of speaking in tongues and any other gift that you would like to bestow on me. I ask this through the power of the Holy Spirit in the name of Jesus Christ. Amen".

PRAYING IN TONGUES

One of the gifts of the Spirit is speaking in tongues. A person can actually be given a spiritual language to speak in. You first have to be baptized in the Holy Spirit to receive this gift.

There is also the gift of the interpretation of tongues. Many people think that tongues should only be spoken in order to be interpreted for the edification of the Church so that people can know what God is saying through tongues. This is not the only use for tongues.

The Holy Spirit can speak in a holy language and pray for the person who is speaking in tongues, or pray for their family, their friends, their neighbours, their Church members, their municipality, their town, their city, their province or state, their country and for the people and the problems of the globe. Imagine the Holy Spirit praying through you!

Do we really know what to pray? So many people are so busy telling God what to do and how to do it. It's arrogant to believe that we could pray a better prayer than the Holy Spirit could pray through tongues through us. This is the greatest value of speaking in tongues. You could be praying for something on your own, completely convinced that you are praying for the right thing, and it could be the exact opposite of the solution God has in mind and you wouldn't even know it.

I think if you have the gift of speaking in tongues, it is something that you should do often. Try to set aside some time every day to pray in the Spirit. It is one of the highest callings to be an intercessor for the Holy Spirit who is the intercessor for the world. Sacrifice some time and energy to pray for God. You can sing in tongues to anointed worship and praise CDs. This can make the experience more enjoyable as you listen to uplifting, beautiful music. Change the atmosphere of your home and the world around you, through praise and worship and through the power of speaking in tongues.

THE POWER OF THE MIND AND MEDITATION

The bible tells us that Jesus knew the thoughts of men.

Matthew 9: 2-6, '2And behold, they brought to him a man sick of the palsy, lying on a bed: and Jesus seeing their faith said unto the sick of palsy; Son, be off good cheer, thy sin be forgiven thee. 3And, behold, certain of the scribes said within themselves, This man blasphemeth. 4And Jesus knowing their thoughts said, "Wherefore think ye evil in your hearts? 5For whether is easier, to say, Thy sins be forgiven thee; or to say, Arise and walk? 6But that ye may know that the Son of Man hath power on earth to forgive sins, (then saith he to the sick of the palsy,) Arise, take up thy bed, and go unto thine house."

Matthew 12:24-25, '24But when the Pharisees heard it, they said, This fellow doth not cast out devils, but by Beelzebub the prince of devils. 25And Jesus knew their thoughts, and said unto them, "Every kingdom divided against itself is brought to desolation; and every city or house divided against itself shall not stand."'

Jesus was able to read people's minds. I think animals can read minds too. People think that animals aren't talking but invisible conversations could be going on. I suspect most creatures can read thoughts. I believe that humans can read thoughts too. If you look at an animal or a person from a distance, they will usually look up at you, like they could feel you looking at them. Have you ever had the feeling that someone or something was watching you? We call it a gut feeling or intuition. We don't know why we instantly don't like someone but later, we may find out why. We don't know why we instantly like someone or even fall in love at first sight, but later, we may find out why. We know so much more than what appears on the surface.

When we think about our thoughts, we think they are inside us. We may not think of them as having any power. Think about when you are nervous when you have to give a speech or think of some activity that would make you nervous if public speaking doesn't do it for you. Now, think about the effects that fear has on you. Your palms may sweat. You may get a dry mouth. Your face may flush. All of that is triggered by the mere thought of having to get up and public speak. To move your fingers or legs or toes, a thought is all it takes. Your body is wired in to your thoughts.

Some co-workers tried an experiment. One after the other, several co-workers spoke to the office receptionist telling her that she didn't look healthy. One asked, "Are you feeling okay? You look under the weather." Another one asked, "Did you get enough sleep last night. You really look tired." Still another said, "I hope you aren't coming down with something. You look really pale." Before long, the receptionist had to go home because she wasn't feeling well.

Our minds are highly suggestible. I remember reading about an experiment in which prisoners of war were told that they would be killed by having all the blood drained out of their bodies. They were blindfolded. A needle was inserted in their arms and instead of blood, warm water was poured down their arms. They thought it was their own blood and they died. They weren't really in danger of dying. They just thought they were so they died anyway.

Another account I heard about was of an elderly lady who was taken to the doctor. The doctor thought she was having symptoms of cancer. An exploratory surgery was planned and the doctor opened her up only to find that she was full of cancerous tumours. Because of her advanced age, the family begged the doctor not to tell the woman about her condition. They felt she had enough to worry about. So, the doctor agreed and instead of telling her how sick she really was, he told her that he had found absolutely nothing wrong and she was totally well.

During the next doctor's visit, it became apparent that the woman no longer had cancer. Apparently, just being told she was healthy was enough of a suggestion that she believed it and it became true for her.

It is along the same lines as what Jesus said about having faith the size of a mustard seed. You could say to a mountain, "be moved into the sea," and if you believed it, it would move into the sea. She believed she was healthy and the cancer cells had to go.

In Matthew 5: 28, Jesus said, "But I say unto you, That whosoever looketh on a woman to lust after her hath committed adultery with her already in his heart."

Thoughts are very powerful. Jesus is basically saying here that if you have even imagined in your mind that you have committed a sin, then you are already guilty of having committed that sin. In the case of rape, I'm sure that a woman who would have been physically raped would be very happy it was only imagined in the mind, but to God, the person is just as guilty. How can that be when actually committing a sin harms someone else so much more than just the thinking about it? Murder is much worse when we actually do it than when we just imagine doing it.

You couldn't be guilty of a crime or a sin unless thoughts have substance outside of you. Just thinking a bad thought about someone, does them a disservice and you do yourself a disservice too.

I know a person who was so angry with someone that they said, "I wish they would just break their arm." And the next day, that person did break their arm.

People can send hate thoughts with an impact. I'm sure Satanic cults have this down to a fine art. Not only can you cause someone to break their arm, you can cause them to drop dead. Voodoo and the black arts are based on this principle of the power of the mind.

Our minds are powerful tools that can be used, both for blessing others and cursing others. Considering that we get back what we give out, do I really have to ask you which you would rather receive back, a blessing or a curse? Let's work on blessing each other. Curses are just merry-go-rounds of pain and suffering that will always come back to haunt you. Isn't it time, we just got off that ride altogether? Remember, if we don't forgive others, God the Father, won't forgive us. It's not worth it!

Meditation and prayer have a great, positive effect on other people. The National Demonstration Program took place in Washington D. C. in June and July of 1993. It brought together 4,000 people to meditate to reduce violent crime in that city. Over the weeks, the number of participants grew and by the end of the study, the number of violent crimes, including rapes, assaults and homicides, had been reduced by 23.3% which coincided with the most number of participants in the meditation. The more the number of people that were meditating increased, the less violent crimes were being committed.

So, not only are you your brother's keeper but you think for the planet too. Cleaning up your thoughts takes on a whole new dimension.

The outside world is wired into your thoughts. For example, if you happened to be a hairdresser, you might notice all the hairstyles of the people around you. If you were a dog trainer, you'd probably notice all the dogs. A dog trainer probably wouldn't notice the hairstyles and a hairdresser probably wouldn't be focussed on the dogs. Each person sees what they are looking for. If you believe that there is always bad news and the world is full of bad people, you'd notice all the bad news and you'd see all the bad people. If you believe that the world is a wonderful place, full of wonderful people, you probably wouldn't see all the bad news. You'd notice all the good news and see all the good people. What you believe is what you see. So, you need to be very careful what you believe. We are all looking for different things as we observe the world around us and we all seem to be able to find what we are looking for.

What do you want to see in your world and in your life? Look for it and you will find it. Jesus said it this way. "Seek and you will find."

In Philippians 4:8, Paul said, "Finally brethren, whatsoever things are true, whatsoever things are honest, whatsoever things are just, whatsoever things are pure, whatsoever things are lovely, whatsoever things are of good report; if there be any virtue, and if there be any praise, think on these things."

It is a good idea to think on good things and to have your mind in a good state. Thinking evil thoughts and dwelling on evil all day long will have a negative effect on you and the world around you.

I don't think that we are being instructed foolishly to ignore the evil around us. I do think it is our responsibility to pray about those negative things and to make every effort to turn them around into good things. However, it is easy to be caught up in the offense and in the evil. The trick is to turn it around into a blessing for yourself and for others.

In Matthew 6: 34, Jesus said, "Sufficient unto the day is the evil thereof." Notice he didn't say, sufficient unto the day is the 'good' thereof. We contribute to the good in our lives and to the good in the world through prayer and thanksgiving to God and through thinking the right thoughts and doing the right actions. This is a classroom, after all, and we are here to learn how to behave. It's a big lesson and God will teach us even if that lesson is painful at times. All things work together for good for those who love the Lord. If you love the Lord, He can turn anything into a blessing.

CHANGING THE WORLD THROUGH OUR RELATIONSHIP WITH MATERIAL POSSESSIONS AND MONEY

I was reading the first several chapters of Matthew in the New Testament and it began to sink in that I had no business calling myself a Christian. I was so far from the mark. So many things that Jesus taught that we shouldn't be doing, I was doing, and things that Jesus taught that I should be doing, I wasn't. I thought I was a Christian and Jesus was my Lord and saviour and yet, I wasn't really following His teachings. Taking up my cross and following Jesus wasn't such an easy thing to do. I guess if it was easy, we'd all be doing it and we'd all be masters of our spirituality by now. I'm sure some people just say to themselves, "I can't measure up to this so I guess I'll just give up now."

I think that God just wants to see that we are at least trying. He has to know we are going to be falling short of the mark in a lot of areas, probably most. I'm not Mother Teresa. Maybe you're not either. But, God still wants us. Trying and failing is much better, in God's eyes, than giving up and not trying at all. Do you give up on your kids every time they make a mistake? I hope you don't. Most likely, you don't. You understand that they are young and that they will make mistakes. God feels the same way about us. We are His children. We are spiritually immature and He knows we are going to make mistakes as we learn. If we could just replace the word 'sin' with the word 'mistake' it would be much clearer what is going on. Sins are just mistakes. God doesn't stop loving you, just because you make mistakes. He knows that it is even necessary for you to make mistakes in order for you to learn from them. No one ever succeeded at anything, except maybe for Jesus, without making a few mistakes along the way. We live. We learn. We grow.

God knew you were going to make mistakes as you learn. He's not surprised. He's not alarmed. He's got you covered. All He expects is for you to at least be trying to improve. Actually, you really can't escape the lessons, no matter who you are or at what level you are in your spiritual journey. The lessons that you need to learn in life, present themselves, one way or the other. Planet earth is a classroom and whether or not you want it to be true, you will be learning through your experiences. You will be getting back whatever you give out. Jesus said you would reap what you sow, Christian or not.

Speaking of reaping what you sow, many evangelists have preached on how important it is to tithe. If you rob God, you will be cursed, but if you pay your tithes to God, you will be blessed.

Malachi 3:8-12, 8'Will a man rob God? Yet ye have robbed me. But ye say, Wherein have we robbed thee? In tithes and offerings. 9Ye are cursed with a curse: for ye have robbed me, even this whole nation. 10Bring ye all the tithes into the storehouse, that there may be meat in mine house, and prove me now herewith, saith the Lord of hosts, if I will not open you the windows of heaven, and pour you out a blessing that there shall not be room enough to receive it. 11And I will rebuke the devourer for your sakes, and he shall not destroy the fruits of your ground; neither shall your vine cast her fruit before the time in the field, saith the Lord of hosts. 12And all nations shall call you blessed: for ye shall be a delightsome land, saith the Lord of hosts.'

Notice God says in this scripture that we have robbed him of both tithes and offerings. I have often heard it preached that we each owe God one tenth of our income. Most Christians, and maybe even some Jews, would probably agree that this should be 10% of your profits after expenses. This 10% is considered to be the tithe. The amount that should be our offerings to God is a little more vague. Someone once told me that all the offerings combined with the tithes found within the bible were added up and they came to a total of about 30% of our profit income. That is a lot more than most preachers, preach.

DREAM ABOUT TITHING THIRTY PERCENT

I had a dream that corresponds with this idea of giving God 30% of our profit income. In the dream, God spoke to me. He said that He wanted the people who could afford it, to tithe 30%. He cautioned me, saying that He only wanted this tithe from the people who could actually afford it. He made it clear that He was not asking people to give more than the 10% if they couldn't afford it.

After having this dream, I asked around if anything written in the bible could justify a 30% tithe and this is when it was explained to me that the tithes and offerings combined in the bible, would add up to somewhere around 30%.

I think it is pretty clear why God would want this 30% from those who can afford it. I'm sure one of the main reasons is that three times the work for God in the world that needs money to fund it, would be funded. A lot more work for the kingdom of God could be done in one third of the time and the time is growing short. Also, according to the tithing principle as described above in Malachi 3, the windows of heaven are going to open up and God is going to pour out a blessing so big, that tithers won't have room to receive it . . . and then they will have more money to tithe.

It is possible that most of us have only been tithing the 10% and missing some of the blessing. We may have needed to be tithing 30% all along to claim the wealth that is promised by God in this scripture.

I hear all the time about the coming wealth transfer. God has promised through modern prophetic words that He will transfer the wealth of the wicked to the righteous. I think this could happen when the righteous start tithing 30% or more than God is requesting. Maybe amazing blessings will happen when we switch with God and give him 90% and ourselves 10%. When you make millions of dollars, how many millions do you actually need after the first few? It's not like our money really belongs to us anyway. If you are a Christian, you may be under the delusion that any of your money actually belongs to you. It all belongs to God.

He gave it to you and He can take it away from you. Keep that in mind as you think about what amount you can afford to tithe.

I know there are probably people who would like to shut me up right about now. They feel 10% is plenty good enough to give to God. Some people don't even give that much. The world doesn't understand the tithing principle. The world believes if you give money away, you lose it. God says if you give it away to Him, He will pay you back. People tithing to God, sounds like the actions of crazy people, to people in the world. Many people live their whole lives just to get more money and to store up treasures on earth. Giving money away is against their religion. If it wasn't tax deductable, they certainly wouldn't do it.

It takes a lot of faith to tithe 30%. God says, in Malachi 3: verse 10, that we can prove Him now herewith, saith the Lord of Hosts, if I will no open you the windows of heaven. He is actually saying we can put Him to the test. I can't think of any other place in the bible where we are told that we can test God to see if He will do what He says He will or not.

If tithing didn't work for you in the past, give it one more try. Tithe 30% and see what happens. Unfortunately, I have also heard it said that if you have robbed God of your tithes and offerings, that it is like back taxes. You still have to pay God back for the robberies of the past years. You may have to tithe a lot before you get God to open those windows. He says, 'bring ye all the tithes into the storehouse' and this could refer to 'all' the tithes, including those owed previously. You could just ask God to forgive your previous debts to Him. The bible says God will forgive your debts if you forgive others their debts unto you. Make sure you have forgiven other people their debts unto you before you go and ask God to forgive you for the tithes and offerings you didn't pay Him. You might have owed Him 30% while you were paying Him only 10%.

At any rate, I don't think you can out give God. Whatever you can spare is a good amount to give. I know it takes a tremendous amount of faith to believe if you are poor. Don't give away everything you have. But, if you can afford to do it, I believe God is asking you to give more. He is also promising to pay you back by opening the windows of heaven and pouring you out a blessing so big that you won't have room to receive it. Put Him to the test. He says you can do that so put Him to the test. Just factor in the 30% you might not have been paying until now and forgive others if you want God to forgive your debts to Him.

I would like to make one more point regarding tithing to God. When you tithe, it is an excellent time to make a request of God. You are giving Him what He wants. It's a very good time to ask Him for what you want. Ask God for whatever it is that you want through the power of the Holy Spirit in the name of Jesus, as you give Him your tithe. Then, envision the blessing that you desire as if it has already happened. Paint a beautiful picture for your subconscious to work on. Keep the end result in your mind. If it's a new house you are asking for, envision the new house and praise God for the new house like you are expecting to receive it. Put a picture of the new house on your fridge and imagine yourself living in that house. Allow yourself to experience and feel how you will feel in your new house. Don't give yourself anxiety by thinking about all the negatives like, how will you get the money to pull this off.

Leave the 'how' in God's hands and just envision the end result. God will do the rest. Your mind is powerful, and God is even more powerful than your mind. The combination of the power of your mind, combined with the power of God, is far reaching. If it's God's will that you get the thing that you desire and it's the right timing, then you will get it.

I was also instructed in a dream to 'praise God in the evening just before going to sleep and to make my requests of God in the morning.' I was told this was a recipe for happiness.

I think most of us tend to think about the worries of the day just as we are about to fall asleep. Many people also tend to watch the news jut before bed and it's usually bad news. These thoughts can keep us tossing and turning, sometimes all night long. The act of praising God before we fall asleep, cleans out the anxiety and fears and sets us up for a good night's sleep. Thinking about all the negatives or thinking poisonous worry thoughts just before we fall asleep, has the opposite effect. So, praise God at night and ask Him for things in the morning, when you can think clearly and when you are rested after a good night's sleep. I believe you will be in a better mood each day if you do this.

Now that the tithing principle has been dealt with to some extent, I'd like to point out a few things about wealth accumulation. Most of us have heard the so called prosperity message based on Malachi 3. However, wealth can be a double edged sword. Yet, the way the prosperity message is preached by some preachers today, you would think that there couldn't possibly be down side to it. Money can become a God and I think money is the most prominent God in the world today. The stomach and the television are close contenders too.

I Timothy 6: 10, 'For the love of money is the root of all evil: which while some coveted after, they have erred from the faith, and pierced themselves through with many sorrows.'

Jesus had a unique take on wealth accumulation as well.

Matthew 6:19-21, '19Lay not up for yourselves treasures upon earth, where moth and rust doth corrupt, and where thieves break through to steal: 20But lay up for yourselves treasure in heaven, where neither moth nor rust doth corrupt, and where thieves do not break through to steal: 21For where your treasure is, there will your heart be also.'

Matthew 19:21 'And behold, one came and said unto him, Good Master, what good thing shall I do, that I may have eternal life? 17And he said unto him, Why callest me good? There is no one good but God: but if thou wilt enter into life, keep the commandments. 18He saith unto him, Which? Jesus said, Thou shalt do no murder, Thou shalt not commit adultery, Thou shalt not steal, Thou shalt not bear false witness, 19Honour thy father and thy mother: and, Thou shalt love thy neighbour as thyself.

20The young man saith unto him, All these things have I kept from my youth up: what lack I yet? 21Jesus said unto him, If thou wilt be perfect, go and sell that thou hast, and give to the poor, and thou shalt have treasure in heaven: and come and follow me.

22But when the young man heard that saying, he went away sorrowful: for he had great possessions.

23Then said Jesus unto his disciples, Verily I say unto you, That a rich man shall hardly enter into the kingdom of heaven. 24And again I say unto you, It is easier for a camel to go through the eye of a needle, than for a rich man to enter into the kingdom of God. 25When his disciples heard it, they were exceedingly amazed, saying, Who then can be saved? 26But Jesus beheld them, and said unto them, With men this is impossible; but with God all things are possible.'

Don't let money become your God. Let God, the father, be your God. Let Jesus Christ rule over your money.

I remember years ago, someone telling me that what I see in other people that I don't like, is probably in me too. I thought this was stupid. Just because I can see a flaw in someone else's personality doesn't mean that I automatically have a similar problem.

I started thinking about this ridiculous theory. At that time, I saw something on the news that really bothered me. A leader of a poverty stricken country was throwing a $100 million dollar birthday celebration for his daughter, while the citizens of his country starved outside his palace gates. I couldn't help but think how many people could have been fed and saved with his $100 million dollars. I also, decided I was absolutely nothing like this man. I would never do something as horrible as that. So, this proved the theory wrong. I asked myself, "Who had I ever let starve while I lavished myself with luxury?"

Then, the realization came to me. I knew there were desperate, starving, dying people in the world. Yet, I spent money on things that I didn't really need. Suddenly, I started to see the similarity between me and this man. Every time I bought another pair of shoes when I could have sent the money to feed the poor, I was choosing to let people starve and die. I discovered I was exactly like this man, perhaps on a smaller scale. If I had his millions of dollars to spend, would there really be much of a difference? I'm sure if I had millions of dollars, I'd want a big, beautiful luxurious home, a new car, money to travel. The list of fun things to buy and do would be endless if I was in that man's tax bracket.

I looked into the mirror and I saw Hitler staring back. It was an epiphany of horror. You see, I thought I was a good person. I went to church. I prayed and I tithed. I tried to be honest and deal fairly with others. All along, I was just some murdering monster who valued shiny bobbles more than human lives.

I was the epitome of evil. Everything Jesus taught us not to do, I was doing. I had stored up treasures on earth to the point of those treasures taking up most of my life, moving them around, weeding, dusting and vacuuming them. Jesus said that whatever I did unto the least of these, I was doing it to Him. I was buying shoes and jewelry while Jesus was suffering and dying overseas . . . and right here at home too.

I wish that I could report that I am now a completely non materialist person who has cleaned out her closets and her life of all of her excess material possessions, but that would be a lie. I'm really struggling with this one and I suspect most other people who live in North America or other affluent nations of the world, are struggling with it too.

Tithing is important just so that we can look at ourselves in the mirror and not loath ourselves. Even if you never do anything else good in this world, it is a good feeling to know that you have sent money to feed families and children or that you have contributed to the digging of fresh water wells that people would die without. Any good cause that you have contributed to, makes you at least feel like maybe you are not a complete waste of space and oxygen. Perhaps you can make the world a better place in some ways even if you aren't perfect. There is no one good but God.

The trick for all of us is to try to keep that account book in good standing. Don't forget 'the least of these.' You may have endless flaws but at least do some good in the world for others. When Jesus divides the sheep, from the goats, based on what they did unto the least of these, make it difficult for him to put you in the goat category. Nobody wants to hear Jesus say, "I never knew you: depart from me, you that work iniquity!" Nobody wants to be sent into everlasting punishment either.

NEW WAYS OF CREATING AND DISPERSING MONEY

As selfish as we can be with our money, we also live in a very flawed world that has a very flawed system for creating and dispensing money. The monetary system, as it stands now, is not very conducive to meeting the needs of local and global populations.

Here's a fact that you probably didn't know about the Bank of Canada. In 1939, Canada was still recovering economically from the first world war and from the stock market crash of 1929 and the great depression that followed. During the depression, there was 30% unemployment and one in five people were on government assistance. In Saskatchewan, due to failed crops, the lowest price for wheat in history and lack of exports, incomes dropped by 90% and 66% of the rural population was living on government relief. Canada was about to enter the second world war but the problem was, Canada didn't have enough money. How was Canada going to pay for this new war? The soldiers had to be equipped and paid. Bullets and guns and bombs and planes had to be built and paid for. The women who stayed at home, had to be paid to work in the ammunition factories. The country was still paying for the first world war. The economy was in the tank and the country could barely feed it's population. What could Canada do when it didn't have the money for all of this?

The government of Canada had the Bank of Canada begin to just print up money out of thin air. You read that right. I'm not lying here. They began just printing up money out of thin air and they started circulating it into the economy. They printed up a ton of money! Suddenly, there was money to pay and equip the soldiers. Suddenly, there was money to pay the women to work in the ammunition factories. Suddenly, there was money to pay for the bullets and the guns and the bombs and the planes and the costs of the first world war. And that's not all. Suddenly, there was money for universal healthcare. Suddenly, there was money for welfare to feed all the starving, desperate people who were unemployed and hungry. Suddenly, there was money for absolutely everything! The economy of Canada boomed during and after the second world war. This money created out of nothing but paper was responsible for it all!

Unfortunately, at the same time as Canada was printing up money, Hitler also got the same brilliant idea. He took a broken down Germany from the brink of bankruptcy after the WWI, to a country that was so wealthy, it almost took over the whole world. This terrified world leaders. They were afraid of the power of this wealth creating tool in the wrong hands.

After WWII, the country of Germany was flooded with counterfeit German money to devalue the German currency and create hyper inflation. The world didn't want Germany to rebuild and they certainly didn't want the general public to know how Hitler had financed his efforts to attain world domination. Unfortunately, the most powerful way in which to save the world and feed the poor and create lives of prosperity for all God's creatures on this earth, was discredited. To this day, the consequences of the actions of Hitler, continue to allow economic conditions that contribute significantly to the destruction of people's lives and the degradation of the environment.

The main problem with our monetary system is that most dollars are created with a debt attached to them in the form of interest. To demonstrate the great evil that interest is, let me give you a couple of examples.

Imagine an island with 10 native people living on it with each person owning one tenth of the island. Now, imagine a banker arriving and offering each one of those people a loan of $10,000. Keep in mind, no money had existed there before. They were just trading with each other for whatever they needed. The banker convinces these ten people to each take out a loan for $10,000. The interest on the loan will be 10% at the end of each year. So, the banker gives each person their $10,000. There is now a total of $100,000 dollars circulating on the island. At the end of the year, it suddenly becomes apparent to these suckers that they have been swindled. At the end of the year, there is still only $100,000 circulating but now each of them owes $1,000 in interest. Where is this additional $10,000.00 that doesn't exist come from? Each person, if they haven't spent all their money, has got to give a $1,000.00 out their original loan of $10,000.00. Now, each of them only has $9,000.00 or less than that if they spent some of the loan money. Let's say, for the sake of the argument, they didn't spend any of the original $10,000.00 The next year, they have to pay another $1,000.00 Now, all they've got left, is $8,000.00 Another 8 years goes by and now, none of these people can afford to pay their loan anymore. The entire $100,000 has been returned to the bank in the form of interest and yet the original $100,000 loan is still owed to the bank. They are all forced into bankruptcy, and the banker now owns the island. These people are in much worse shape then they ever could have been before the banker. They no longer have a home or an income and they are desolate and destroyed. They have no where to go. They have no food to eat and no money to buy food even if they had money.

Although simplistic, this is exactly how interest works. Could anything be more wicked?

Here's another example. According to William Hixon, in his book, 'The Triumph of the Bankers,' the cost to Britain of the war of 1812 with the US was $500 million dollars. Britain has paid interest for over 200 years on the cost of that war. They have paid $4 billion dollars in interest on that original war and the $500 million owed on that war that took place over 200 years earlier, is still outstanding. Can you imagine a more corrupt system then this? This is the very same monetary system that Canada and the US and the world are still under. Is there anyone in the world who thinks this is just and fair to the taxpaying citizens of Britain or to any other citizen of any other country that is struggling under this kind of tyranny. No wonder governments around the globe are having problems helping their citizens when most of their money has to go straight to the banks in the form of interest payments. If it weren't for being allowed to run deficits to finance the debts, every country in the world would go bankrupt instantly.

Africa's debt costs more money to fund yearly then it's government can afford to spend on the health and the education of its population yearly and it is one of the poorest countries in the world. It's criminal what is going on. Hitler is alive and well and still killing the most vulnerable people in society. If our taxes weren't being spent to finance this terrorism in the world, just think what could be accomplished for the greater good of mankind! It's time we got this gorilla off of our backs!

God has a plan for eliminating interest. God declared in the bible that all debts should be forgiven, every fifty years! It was called the Year of Jubilee and the conditions are described in Leviticus chapter 25. All the slaves were freed and all the debts were forgiven. If we want our world to be healed, it's time we had another Year of Jubilee. Debt forgiveness seems like an oxymoron. Who really should be forgiving who here? Do the bankers need to forgive us our debts unto them or should we be putting them all in jail for their monstrous actions of tyranny against us?

The operative word here is 'forgive.' Forgive debts and forgive trespasses. One way or another, this interest problem must come to an end or it will be the death of all of us. It can't be allowed to continue. We are under Satan's monetary system. It is oppressive and destructive. It will eventually destroy the earth. God's monetary system is liberating and prosperous. If implemented, it can save the earth.

Even one seed, from one apple, from one tree, can produce a tree, that has many more apples, that can produce many more seeds, that can produce many more apple trees and so on and so on. God's system of provision is infinitely prosperous. Money created without interest attached to it can produce results similar to the endless provision of God found in one apple seed.

Some interesting quotes of famous people are to follow. All of these quotes, 1-5, I found in a little known underground newspaper, called the Michael Journal. It was (and still may be operational) published in Rougemount, Quebec in 1994 and 1995.

1Henry Ford proposed government created interest free money for the Muscle Shoals hydro electric station on the Tennessee River.

The American inventor, Thomas Edison, agreed with Henry Ford's proposal. He stated, "They (the debt free bills) will be based on the public wealth already in Muscle Shoals: they will be retired by the earnings and power of the dam. That is, the people of the United States will have all that they put into Muscle Shoals and all that they can take out for centuries . . . the endless wealth making power of the Tennessee River . . . with no tax and no increase in the national debt."

"It is absurd to say that our country can issue $30 million in bonds but not $30 million in currency. Both are promises to pay, but one fattens the usurers (banks) and the other helps the people. If the currency issued by the government was no good, then the bonds would be no good either. It is a terrible situation when the government, to increase the national wealth, must go into debt and submit to ruinous interest rates at the hands of men who control the fictitious value of gold."

2MacKenzie King, Prime Minister of Canada, had the following to say about the banks. "Once a nation parts with control of its currency and credit, it matters not who makes that nation's laws. Usury, once in control, will wreck any nation. Until the control of the issue of currency and credit is restored to government and recognized as its most conspicuous and sacred responsibility, all talk of sovereignty of Parliament and democracy is idle and futile . . ."

3President Abraham Lincoln issued debt-free greenbacks to conduct the Civil War in 1862. He was re-elected in 1864, after promising to attack the power of the bankers as soon as the war was over.

Lord Goschen, a spokesman for the financiers and the director of the Bank of England, wrote in the London Times in 1865, "If this mischievous financial policy, which has it's origin in North America, shall become indurated down to a fixture, then that government will furnish its own money without cost. It will pay off debts and be without debt. It will have all the money necessary to carry on its commerce. It will become prosperous without precedent in the history of the world. That government must be destroyed, or it will destroy every monarchy on the globe."

3Abraham Lincoln was assassinated on April 14th of the same year as this statement by Lord Goschen was published. A tremendous restriction of credit followed in the US, organized by the banks, that decreased the amount of currency in circulation by almost 66%, and within ten years, 56,446 businesses went bankrupt losing collectively $2 billion. In 1887, the banks further reduced that to an amount representing a reduction in money of almost 90% of what it had been when Lincoln was president. (Keep in mind, that there was practically no unemployment or any bankruptcies in the US prior to this interference by the banks. As described by Lord Guschen, the US would have become prosperous without precedent in the history of the world . . . if the banks hadn't stopped them.)

4Graham Towers, who was Governor of the Bank of Canada, 1935-1954, was asked the following question before the House of Commons Standing Committee on Banking and Commerce in 1939.

"Will you tell me why a government with the power to create money should give that power away to a private monopoly and then borrow that which parliament can create itself back at interest to the point of national bankruptcy?"

Towers replied, "Now, if parliament wants to change the form of operating the banking system, then certainly that is within the power of parliament."

In 1939, the government told the Bank of Canada to start printing up money out of nothing, which it did, and all the money needed to pay for WWII, etc. was created.

Furthermore, unless there have been changes made to Canada's Bank Act, Canada's federal government still has the right to do this even today. Unfortunately, the United States government no longer owns its central bank. However, where there is a will, there still might be a way, if people are determined to free themselves from oppression and tyranny.

Paul Hellyer, who was Deputy Prime Minister of Canada, wrote a book called, 'Funny Money.' It is one of the most informative books I have ever read on the topic of money and finance. He suggests some excellent ideas for discussion on how we can change our world by changing our monetary policies. I highly recommend that anyone read this book who has an interest in changing our world through improving our monetary system. Mr. Hellyer does a great job of exposing corruption in high places as well as proposing practical solutions to economic problems.

Paul Heller does not feel that banks should be abolished altogether. He thinks it would be better to establish strict rules of conduct and explicit guidelines and use the existing medium rather than replace banking institutions with government institutions that might be less efficient at performing their function. He advocates a decentralized banking system with their existing interest bearing formula as a source of income. The banks would create 50% of the new money with interest, while the government would create 50% of the new money without interest. This would not create inflation because the banks would be creating less money while the government would be creating more but the same amount of money would still be produced. It would, however, reduce interest over time and eventually halt the escalating debt and deficit.

Jordan Grant, president of Seaton group and chairman of the Bank of Canada for Canadians Coalition, has been speaking up for the concept of debt-free money. He suggested financing the Liberal government's $6 billion infrastructure program by borrowing the entire amount from the Bank of Canada at no interest. He suggested that it could be looked at as an experiment to see to what extent we should be shifting government money creation and borrowing into the hands of the Bank of Canada and away from the private banking system. That's one way to eliminate a lot of interest in a hurry.

Jack Biddell, a Canadian accountant, suggested that the Bank of Canada create loans at interest rates of only 1%, to be used by either provincial or federal governments to exchange high interest debt for low interest debt or for infrastructure projects.

Paul Hellyer agrees with both Grant and Biddell and he would like to see these ideas applied on a much larger scale making interest free money available for every legitimate government financial need. However, he cautions that too much of a good thing all at once can kill you. Hellyer calls for cautious implementation over a period of time.

Paul Hellyer states in his book, that almost all religions call on its members to take care of those less fortunate than themselves. He asks the question, "What is the moral judgement of economic policies that reduce the creation of wealth by trillions of dollars when there are needy outstretched hands from one corner of the globe to the other."

He points out that one in every four children born in the Third World dies before the age of five. Every year, over 10 million people die from impure water, malnutrition and lack of immunization against diseases. He states, "The world's indifference is the silent tragedy."

Let's not be indifferent. Let's do something. Let's look at LETS.

LETS

We've talked about the problems that too much interest is causing in the world. Here's a very interesting idea which has the potential to generate untold amounts of wealth while also eliminating wealth creation that is tied to interest. LETS stands for 'Local Exchange Trading System.'

It essentially runs like a barter system. However, the problem with a barter system, is that I may be a hairdresser and you are a well digger. If you don't need a haircut and I don't need a well dug, then a trade won't take place.

With a LETS, each person is give a certain number of credits in the system for performing a skill or trade. These credits are the 'money' that is exchanged. The best thing about these credits is that they are created without any debt attached to them. Interest is eliminated. Also, no so-called 'real' dollars from the world outside are needed for the system to generate wealth for its members. The LETS generates it's own currency and is interest free. So, I cut someone's hair and I get maybe 20 credits in the system for doing that. Then, I can buy 20 credits worth of service or product from another member of the LETS. That way, everyone can trade with everyone without being limited to just an exchange between two people as in the barter system.

This kind of system would be particularly effective in poor regions in third world countries where actual dollars don't even exist to be circulating and stimulating the economy. They don't have any money and their neighbours don't have any money either. Does it really make sense to have plumbers and contractors and carpenters be out of work or to have people live without a roof over their heads when there are people who are ready and willing to build those houses and people ready and willing to buy those houses? The only thing lacking is a means of exchange, 'money.' Someone isn't doing their job of making sure that enough money is circulating to allow this commerce to take place. LETS is a method of making 'money' or credits out of actual labour and allowing commerce to take place where otherwise it couldn't, due to a lack of funds.

Unfortunately, people in developed countries such as Canada and the US, don't completely comprehend what a shortage of money is all about or comprehend how damaging interest can be. They have money and they can probably get some more money. People aren't dying due to a lack of dollars circulating around them to the extent that they are in developing nations. They may feel the pinch here but they really don't seem to fully comprehend the benefits of a LETS. Nevertheless, some activity is happening in the area of local currencies, called 'community currencies' in North America and around the globe. With barter services and community currencies, in the U.S. alone, billions of dollars annually are being exchanged in this manner and many more billions worldwide. It's a small start in the right direction.

If you are interesting in learning more about LETS, you can research it on the internet. One useful website that I found can be accessed here. **http://www.gmlets.unet.com/**

HOW TO PROTECT YOURSELF AND OTHERS FOR A BRIGHTER FUTURE

SUMMARY

How do we protect ourselves individually and collectively from the hardships that will come upon this earth? A lot of suggestions have already been made. I didn't feel that I should go too deeply into the details but instead, I wanted to present a general overview of a lot of ideas and principles of spirituality.

Yes. The protection of God is lifting off of Canada and the United States and around the globe and it is not a coincidence. God's personality and His rules for successful living are still the same. The ten commandments are still in force. They are not the ten suggestions.

If we want God to return His protection to us, we must comply with His requirements.

Exodus 20:1-17, '1And God spake all these words, saying, 2 I am the Lord thy God, which have brought thee out of the land of Egypt, out the house of bondage. 3Thou shalt have no other gods before me. 4 Thou shalt not make any likeness of any thing that is in heaven above, or that is in the earth beneath, or that is in the water under the earth: 5Thou shalt not bow down thyself to them, nor serve them: for I the Lord thy God am a jealous God, visiting the iniquities of the fathers upon the children unto the third and fourth generation of them that hate me;

6And shewing mercy unto thousands of them that love me, and keep my commandments. 7Thou shalt not take the name of the Lord thy God in vain; for the Lord will not hold him guiltless who taketh his name in vain. 8Remember the Sabbath day, to keep it holy. 9Six days shalt thou labour and do all they work:

10But the seventh day is the sabbath of the Lord thy God: in it thou shalt not do any work, thou, nor thy son, nor thy daughter, thy manservant, nor thy maidservant, nor thy cattle, nor they stranger that is within thy gates: 11For in six days the Lord made heaven and earth, the sea, and all that in them is, and rested the seventh day: wherefore the Lord blessed the Sabbath day and hallowed it.

12Honour thy father and thy mother: that thy days may be long upon the land which the Lord thy God giveth thee. 13Thou shalt not kill. 14Thou shalt not commit adultery. 15Thou shalt not steal. 16 Thou shalt not bear false witness against thy neighbour. 17Thou shalt not covet thy neighbour's house, thou shalt not covet thy neighbour's wife, nor his manservant, nor his maidservant, nor his ox, nor his ass (donkey,) nor any thing that is thy neighbour's.

There are some strong commandments in here. They are still important to God. Luckily, we have Jesus to help us obey them and to forgive us if we get it wrong. Nevertheless, pay particular attention that you are trying to do these ten commandments.

The general population no longer pays attention or really cares what God wants. They are breaking these commandments. They have many idols and gods before God, including food, wine, money, worldly possessions and television, to name just a few. Some people take the Lord's name in vain every day of the week, several times a day, and don't even know they are speaking a curse down on their heads. It's business as usual on Sundays with everyone shopping and a lot of people working. Making money is more important to the stores that stay open. Children do not honour their parents. Disrespect of all authority figures is rampant in our society. It seems no one wants anyone to tell them what to do, especially God. Thou shalt not kill <u>does</u> apply to abortions. Fifty-five million deaths cry out to the Lord for justice. It seems that adultery is almost an accepted activity in today's world. The world is full of liars and those who bear false witness. I've been to court and heard it with my own ears. Even Christians will swear on the bible and then they will tell lies about everything that happened to wiggle out of the legal consequences of their actions. Thieves are running amuck. They are not interested in working at an honest job for an honest wage when it so much easier to just steal what they want. They believe the world owes it to them. Coveting is a national past-time. Every commercial on TV is geared to make you covet one thing or another so that you will buy it. People never seem to be satisfied. They want more and more and more and the advertisers and the merchandisers are more than happy to oblige.

The problem is we have turned away from God with our behaviour. He will not tolerate us forever. He is now warning people that bad things are about to happen if they don't repent and change their ways. This is a scenario that has repeated throughout the bible many times. God warns the people. If they repent and change their ways, He will have mercy on them. If they are stubborn and rebellious and refuse to turn from their evil ways, then the lesson will arrive on our proverbial doorsteps. God will not be mocked.

If you are not a Christian, you need to accept Jesus into your life as your Lord and saviour. How can you truly succeed in life without the help of the Master? You need to ask for forgiveness and obey God. If you are not baptized in the Holy Spirit, you need to have this experience so that you will have the wisdom and the power of God on your side, to help you and to help others.

The next thing you need to do is trust God. Yes. Terrible things may be on the way but remember that God is perfectly capable of taking care of you no matter what happens. He will provide protection for you. He might provide a shelter in a remote area or He might just stop the bullets in mid air. If there is a shortage of food, remember that Jesus fed five thousand people with just a bit of bread and a few fishes. He can still do that. Remember, all things work together for good for those who love the Lord. ALL THINGS! Even terrorist attacks and wars and famines can all be turned around for your good. God will provide for His children in all these things. God can even prevent all these things from happening if enough people will repent and change. But, if this judgement must come upon this wicked generation, God will look after His people through it all.

If you have the money and the means to get a cottage or to set up a place of refuge off the beaten trail somewhere, then you can do that. Maybe you can even find a community of like minded Christian people to move into. You can pick a place with a good water source, store up food, buy a solar powered generator or have the place outfitted with solar power. Wind turbines can also be set up to generate power. You can even store up weapons and bullets. It's not illegal to do that . . . at least not yet. You can grow your own food, plant some apple trees and other perennial plants that would make a good source of food. If everything shuts down and trucks can't get or carry gas, food, water or other supplies or the electricity goes off, you'll be ready. If millions of people are suddenly without a food or water supply, you'll be very glad you planned ahead. The point isn't to live in fear and prepare for the worst. The point is to trust God and just in case, have a contingency plan.

There are many websites on the internet that you can research that can tell you how to get ready for emergencies such as power outages. You really should spend some time looking up what you need to do to be ready because we do know that 'trouble' is coming. Remember that gut feeling I was talking about. Most people's guts are telling them that something very bad is on the way. Having flashlights and batteries and candles or oil burning lamps can make life a lot easier. Store up water. The average person uses 70 gallons of water a day when you take into consideration a shower and cooking. You might want to have a few gallons a day, set aside for an emergency. Having some rain barrels to collect water in is a good idea too. Water can mould or get bacteria in it, so you would want to keep drinking it and replenishing a fresh supply. Store up food. Canned goods can last quite a while and so can dried goods such as grains and legumes. Even dried fruits, seeds and nuts can last a very long time. You can purchase freeze dried food and some of these can last up to 20-30 years. You can start stocking up a supply now. I would think that you would want to store at least a few months worth of food to feed yourself and your family in a crisis. Having a few buckets of freeze dried foods for an extended crisis is also a really good idea.

Any time after December 21, 2012, 'trouble' is coming for the world. I believe it is the beginning of a time of testing that will continue until the anti-Christ is in power. It will be a very difficult time so prepare. If I'm wrong about all of this, at least you will have peace of mind knowing that if a crisis does present itself, you are ready. Knowing that you have prepared, has got to relieve some of the anxiety you might have regarding future events that you may have very little control over at the time they happen. On that note, getting out of the stock market might be a good idea for the average person. Trouble in the world can affect the price of stocks. Unless you are an expert, who knows when to get in and when to get out or how to play the stock market in difficult times, you should probably leave the stock market to the professionals. I think it's going to be a steep roller coaster ride from now on.

To improve your health and to make the world a better place to live for the poor who are starving from a lack of food, consider becoming a vegetarian. Many more people can be fed world wide if most people were vegetarians. A lot of animals can be spared lives of torture ending in cruel deaths too. If enough people eat raw foods, who knows what effect this could have on world peace? Buy organic. Don't support the pesticide industry unless you think that's the healthiest way to go.

Remember to pray about everything and remember to praise God in all circumstances. If you can pray in tongues, pray and worship often in tongues. This may be one of the highest forms of prayer there is. Remember, when you pray to not believe that you know better than God and tell Him what to do and how to do it. Always end your prayers with, "If it be Your will, Lord." Don't seek your own will and your solution, but His will and His solution.

If you see Muslims, pray for their souls to be saved. God told me through a dream to pray for people's eyes to be opened and their hearts to be softened. I have heard accounts of Jesus appearing to Muslims and saving them. Pray for them and Jesus can and will save them.

Try to think higher thoughts. Limit your television programs and the time you spend in front of the TV. Spend more time with God. Remember, you think for the globe. Clean up your thoughts and clean up the world.

It is very important that Christians reach out to more people than just the people on their own streets and in their own neighbourhoods and in their own Churches. We need to reach the whole globe for a solution that will work for all of us. If you can tithe the 30% that God is asking for from some of us, then this will undoubtedly increase the ability of the Christian charities to help many more people. Much more work can be done for God in a shorter time.

When you help others, you are helping yourself. And when you reach out to the neediest in society, you are doing it unto Jesus. See Jesus everywhere and treat Him good. This can only come back to you in the very best of ways. Give out blessings. Give out forgiveness. Give out peace. These things will come back to you. If you want a better world for yourself and for your children, then you must improve the world for others. It is the law of reaping what you sow. It is a very fair law. If you give it out, you get it back. Cause and effect. Action and reaction.

Your life has meaning. Everything you do has an effect. Make a big splash! Change the world! With God's help and direction, through the power of the Holy Spirit, in the name of Jesus Christ, you can do it! We can do it!